CREASE+FOLD

CREASE+FOLD

Innovative **Origami Projects** Anyone Can Make

SOK SONG

FOREWORD BY MICHAEL LAFOSSE AND RICHARD ALEXANDER

Photographs by Alexandra Grablewski

POTTER CRAFT

New York

Published in the United States by Potter Craft, an imprint of the
Crown Publishing Group, a division of Random House, Inc., New York.
www.crownpublishing.com
www.pottercraft.com

POTTER CRAFT and colophon is a registered trademark of
Random House, Inc.

Library of Congress Cataloging-in-Publication Data

Song, Sok.
Crease and fold : innovative origami projects anyone
can make / by Sok Song.
    p. cm.
 Includes index.
 ISBN 978-0-307-58651-3
 1. Origami. I. Title.
 TT870.S6643 2010
 736′.982--dc22
 2010006661

Printed in China

PHOTOGRAPHY BY ALEXANDRA GRABLEWSKI

PHOTOGRAPHY ON PAGE 117 BY RODERICK MICKENS/AMNH. COURTESY OF THE
AMERICAN MUSEUM OF NATURAL HISTORY.

ALL ILLUSTRATIONS BY SOK SONG, EXCEPT THOSE ON PAGES 67-9, 75-77,
83-85, 96, 119-120, AND 123 BY FRANCES SOOHOO.

DESIGN BY CHALKLEY CALDERWOOD

TECHNICAL EDITING BY MARCIO NOGUCHI

10 9 8 7 6 5 4 3 2

First Edition

This book is dedicated to
Alexus and Evelyn Song,
my two darling
and beautiful nieces.

CONTENTS

Origami 101

Foreword

In the last few decades, paper-folding designs have rapidly evolved with highly technical and often mathematical influences. This advent of the complex has stolen the spotlight from a world of simpler folds, fondly ingrained in the minds of many origami designers.

- -

This book presents a generous collection of origami projects that remind us how elegant the simple models can be. Sok has prepared a selection of designs you will find fun and refreshing, unusual in their elegance and comfortably within the reach of all folding enthusiasts. He has not forgotten the struggle that the novice may face when first learning origami from books.

For years Sok has shown the origami community he has a special touch, or flair, that makes his exquisitely folded projects rise above the rest. His greeting cards, which showcase his innovative designs and an attention to high-quality materials, have won him many fans throughout the world. Just as important, Sok is a wonderful teacher and has always been a cheerful promoter of the art of origami. This book faithfully represents him in this regard, and you are sure to be inspired.

Michael LaFosse & Richard Alexander
Origamido Studio

Introduction

O rigami is beautiful, and timeless, thanks to its simplicity. After all, there is only one way to fold a piece of paper. Yet within that single fold is a universe of possibilities. With every variation of a fold, a new shape emerges. In a common sheet of paper, there exists the notion of a flower, the thought of a fish, and the dream of a bird.

- -

Origami is an ancient art, and its history stretches across thousands of years. It has crossed boundaries of language and culture. Its practitioners are young and old. It has survived, thrived, and made millions of ordinary people into artists. Every generation, indeed every person who folds, has made a contribution to origami.

But even though the history of paper folding dates back to the invention of paper, as a recognized art form it is fairly young. The basic techniques of this craft are constant (a crease here, a fold there), but origami is very much a living, breathing, changing art. In fact, modern origami has come a long way from the days when it was used as a ceremonial tradition or children's craft, thanks to the variety of people who fold paper. While some folders are content to create the simple but beautiful crane thousands of times, others prefer to experiment and uncover new, exotic forms and techniques: tessellations that undulate and repeat, modular geometric shapes that utilize underlying mathematical principles, wet folds that come to life when dampened with water, and complicated models that take hours of delicate work and concentration. It is this variety of ideas, techniques, and models that make modern origami so appealing to such a wide variety of people.

In fact, my own models are another example of the variety you find in the world of origami. While many are inspired by traditional designs, bases, and folds, they are all one-of-a-kind and expressions of my style as an origami artist.

This book is organized by the size of the projects, and encompasses my journey and career working with this diverse medium. We'll start with the fundamentals of origami, basic folds and bases, and then explore my unique versions of the animals that have delighted people for so many generations. With these projects you will be able to make cards, jewelry, and other small, fun projects. Then we'll move on to another popular type of origami: folding useful objects and decorative items. These medium-sized pieces will help give you an idea of how origami can be used for fashion and home decor. Last but certainly not least, the final section includes instructions for a few larger pieces that might surprise you. From giant elephants, to full-sized lampshades and origami handbags, I have tried to include a little bit of everything from the world of origami.

By the end of this book, you may just find that origami itself has transformed in your mind. What you once thought of as a simple hobby with specialized paper might turn into an art form that draws on many new and recycled materials to touch the worlds of fashion design, home decor, craft, and fine art. All you need is some interest, practice, and a piece of paper to crease and fold.

Foldingly Yours,
Sok Song

Origami 101

As you might guess, sloppy folding results in a sloppy finished model. My friends and I jokingly call this style of folding "mushy-gami." Making crisp, neat folds can sometimes be a challenge, but with patience and practice it is possible for anyone to make them—and to make beautiful origami. The following section will show and explain the most common symbols, folds, and bases used in origami. A command of these origami terms will help you create the models in this book (and beyond).

Symbols and Folds

Developed by Akira Yoshizawa and refined by Samuel Randlett, the standard set of origami symbols and notations for diagramming allows you to see the steps of a model visually. Some people believe folding diagrams should stand alone, conveying the entire folding sequence without words. Since the symbols are universal, instructions that can stand alone make it possible for crafters to use foreign origami books without having to translate the text descriptions. However, other origami artists believe that a good set of diagrams should also have corresponding textual descriptions (so the instructions can be dictated verbally). For the diagrams in this book, I tried to follow both these schools of thought: The illustrations should guide you through a project on their own, but they are all accompanied by text as well.

SYMBOLS

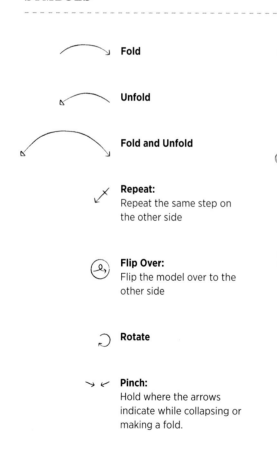

Fold

Unfold

Fold and Unfold

Repeat:
Repeat the same step on the other side

Flip Over:
Flip the model over to the other side

Rotate

Pinch:
Hold where the arrows indicate while collapsing or making a fold.

View:
Indicates the next illustration will show the model from a different vantage point.

Magnify:
Indicates the next illustration will show a close-up view of the same step.

Focal Points:
These circles will help you match up one part of a model to another when making a fold without clear landmarks.

FOLDS

Fold (Valley Fold):
Fold up or down along red dashed line.

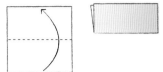

Mountain Fold:
Fold over or under along blue dashed and dotted line.

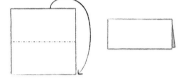

Inside Reverse Fold:
Fold corner or flap inside layers reversing one of the creases to help make it happen.

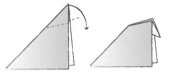

Outside Reverse Fold:
Fold corner or flap on the outside reversing one of the creases to help make it happen.

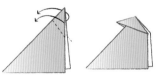

Pleat:
Fold and then fold back shorter than before to create a pleat.

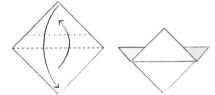

Squash Fold:
Open the pocket and squash flat.

Swivel Squash Fold:
Swivel the paper to the side while opening the pocket to squash flat.

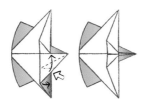

Rabbit Ear Fold:
Fold two diagonals at the same time to bring out a point or flap like the ear of a rabbit.

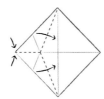

Collapse:
Using existing creases collapse the model into a base or shape in preparation for the next step.

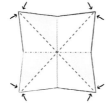 

Tuck:
A tuck is just a small version of the Inside Reverse Fold. It's generally used to blunt a corner or hide a point on a model.

Magnified

Stress-Free Folding

1. Read the instructions carefully before making a fold. It helps to look ahead at the next diagram to see where you are going.

2. Always remember to fold on a smooth, hard surface. Working on a soft surface makes it difficult to fold crisply and precisely.

3. Fold firm for strong creases. The neater and crisper the fold, the better the final model will come out. You want to avoid getting mushy-gami!

4. Don't panic! Origami is meant to be very relaxing and calming. When you have trouble with a step, take a deep breath and review the instructions or try again from the beginning. If you really get stuck and can't go any further, there are people who can help you. Just look for a local origami club or search on the Internet. There are a lot of origami enthusiasts willing to help—so send an e-mail or reach out if you're in need of some advice.

5. Practice makes perfect. Don't worry if your first try isn't the most beautiful origami you've ever seen. Even the most advanced folders have to practice a model several times before getting it right. I often fold a model repeatedly until I feel satisfied with the finished product. As a bonus, repeating the same model time and again helps reinforce the sequence of folds and develop muscle memory—eventually you'll be able to fold a model without the diagrams in front of you!

6. Share the joy! Just as I am sharing my passion for folding with you, pass it on to someone you know—or even someone you don't know. Fold in the waiting room or while riding a bus or train (but not while driving!). After you fold a model you like, give it as a gift to somebody, put it in a card, or fold a tip for your server. They will surely appreciate it, and they may even ask you to teach them how to do it. Friends who visit my home sometimes are surprised when they don't see a lot of folded objects. That's because almost everything I fold is given away to others. This is just my way of sharing the joy of origami.

In this photo you can see how a model changes when folded with different sizes of paper. From top to bottom, these elephants are folded from 15", 10", 6", and 3" paper.

Choosing the Right Paper

One of the great things about origami is that you can find the right project for almost any type of paper. But even though the choices for paper are vast, using the right paper for a particular project is essential when you are just starting out or when you are trying to create beautiful pieces of origami art.

Luckily, there are a lot of commercially available papers on the market made especially for origami. The choices range from the cheap and traditional onionskin paper called kami to the more expensive and durable Japanese washi, and everything in between!

Traditional origami paper comes in various sizes. The standard size is a 6″ (15cm) square, and other common sizes measure 3″, 10″, and 15″(7.5cm, 25.5cm, and 38cm) square. Most models can be folded from the standard 6″ (15cm) square, but oftentimes complex models are easier to fold if you use a larger size. The smaller 3″ (7.5cm) size is generally used for modular origami, which requires multiple sheets. If you are using paper that was not made for origami, you should use a paper cutter to square it off to a conventional size.

Before each project's instructions I will discuss the various paper options that would work best for a particular model. For example, sometimes the look you want for the resulting model depends on a specific color or type of paper. However, I also recommend that you "fold outside the box" and experiment on your own with different papers. With some practice, you will soon have a better sense of what papers you enjoy working with, and you will be able to choose the perfect paper for a specific model on your own!

Here are brief descriptions of some of the most common papers used for origami (check out the Resources section in the back of this book for stores and websites where these papers can be found):

1. Kami: There are many brands of kami, which is the name for traditional onionskin paper with a bright color on one side and white on the other. It is the most economical and common paper for origami on the market.

2. Mono Paper: Mono paper has the same color on both sides. There are many brands and types available. Memo cubes are probably the most common—and cheapest—way to buy mono paper. It's common for mono paper to be sold in large sheets that must be cut to a traditional size.

3. Duo Paper: Duo paper has different colors on each side. There are many different brands of these papers available as well. Many scrapbooking papers are printed with different colors and prints on each side; if you cut them to a traditional size you can make your own duo paper!

4. Foil Paper: This type of paper is readily available, and it can be great for folding because it's very thin and flexible. However, there is also a drawback: Once a crease has been made with foil paper, it is difficult to undo, and the paper

will always show the crease you made (and thus any imperfections). Foil is great to use for folding practice and when designing new models because of its malleability. If you go shopping after Christmas, you may get lucky and find a whole roll of foil wrapping paper that you can then cut to size!

5. Washi: The name of this paper tells you where it came from! *Wa* means "Japanese" and *shi* translates to "paper." Washi is more than just an average sheet of Japanese paper though; it is a strong, fibrous paper perfect not only for a lot of origami models, but also other traditional crafts and art. It comes in various colors and prints and is often smooth on one side and textured on the other.

6. Print Chiyogami: Typically sold in a variety pack, print chiyogami is a thin paper, typically kami, that has been printed on one side with a pattern. Since it is commercially printed by machine, it is usually very affordable despite the complexity of the designs.

7. Yuzen Chiyogami: This paper is the deluxe version of print chiyogami. Yuzen chiyogami is usually silk-screened or block-printed by hand with beautiful floral and traditional kimono patterns. It often uses bright, bold color combinations and special metallic inks. It can come in large 2' × 3' (61cm × 91cm) sheets or in smaller precut squares for origami.

8. Recycled and Alternative Papers: I repurpose paper all the time, often because I don't have origami paper with me when I travel. But sometimes I recycle because inspiration strikes: A certain print in a magazine or a particular pattern on a poster intrigues me, and I can't help but fold it! I encourage you to start thinking the same way. I know you can turn those piles of paper around the house into origami treasures. Chances are you have plenty of suitable paper handy, whether it's gift wrap, old calendars, maps, envelopes, or leftover wall paper. You can also personalize recycled paper by painting on it, making a paper collage, or photocopying an old letter. Using these alternative papers can be extremely satisfying—some of my favorite projects were made with repurposed paper!

THE FINEST PAPER OF ALL: HANDMADE PAPER AT ORIGAMIDO STUDIO

Making paper by hand is an involved process, but the results can surpass the quality of paper made by machine. Michael LaFosse and Richard Alexander are two of the leaders in the field, and their studio, Origamido, is known for making some of the best origami paper in the world. Their sheets are sought after by major origami masters and paper artists alike.

As you might expect, Michael and Richard have the art of making paper down to a well-rehearsed routine. When I visited their studio, they took me through the whole thing, step by step. Here's the story of my day "behind the scenes."

First, beaten pulp goes into a large machine where it is crushed and mixed with water. Origamido's recipe for origami paper includes a combination of long, thin, strong fibers including abaca, cotton, linen, and hemp. Once the pulp reaches the right consistency, it is put into a vat of water where it is colored and conditioned with various dyes and mica powders. It's a magical process, mixing colors into the paper pulp—you draw on all you know about combining primary colors to make new colors. There is a point when the pulp hasn't quite fully combined when the multi-colored combination creates interesting patterns with spots of color. I learned that sometimes the mixing stops at this stage so the paper maker can create patterns or blocks of color on the finished paper.

Next, a screen is submerged in the mixture and then pulled up in a swooping motion, dredging the fibers onto the screen. Michael and Richard use different types of screens to make their origami paper: a standard Western-style screen and a Japanese bamboo screen. Each screen has a different mesh and gives the finished paper a different texture.

If the layer of pulp on the screen is smooth enough, it is transfered straight to a cloth on the blotting and drying mat so the moisture can be absorbed. The drying mats are then stacked and put under a weighted press to squeeze out the excess water. The pressure takes out most of the moisture, but the stack must go into a drying system overnight to remove the water that remains. The moment the sheets of paper come out of the drier the next day is so rewarding. It's amazing to see, and then use, strong, beautiful papers you made with your own hands.

Hopefully one day I will have my own paper making studio!

Origami Base-ics

In origami, a "base" is a common starting point for almost any model you create. There are many bases, but the ones that follow are some of the most common—and also the only ones that will be used in this book.

For all the bases that follow, starting with the white side (or back side) of your paper face up will create a colored base. Some projects in this book may tell you to start with a base where the white side—rather than the colored side—is face out. When that happens, you would fold one of the bases below, starting with the white side face down instead.

If this your first time folding the bases, practice them all several times before moving on to the projects in the following chapters. Once you master the bases, you will have a stronger origami foundation, and it will be much easier to fold the origami models. If you are already familiar with origami bases, you may notice that some of the folding sequences differ from traditional methods—these are simply changes I've made over the years with the input of my many origami students.

TRIANGLE BASE

We start with the simple Triangle Base. Some people argue that this is more a fold than a base; however, I see it as the starting point for many traditional models, and that is what defines a base.

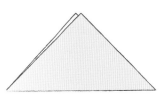

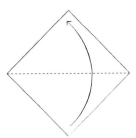

1. Fold in half, bottom to top.

FINISHED TRIANGLE BASE!

WATERBOMB BASE

This base received its name because many of the traditional models that are made from it are inflatable with air or water. With water-resistant paper, it is possible to make a paper version of the water balloon!

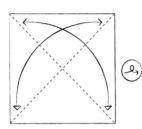

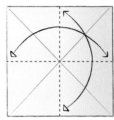

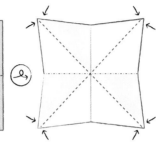

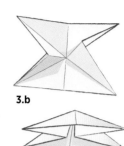

3.b

3.c

1. Fold in half, corner to corner, in both directions. Unfold. Flip over.

2. Fold in half, edge to edge, in both directions. Unfold. Flip over.

3.a Pinch all 4 corners and collapse along the fold lines.

FINISHED WATERBOMB BASE!

KITE BASE

The Kite Base—also called the Ice Cream Cone Base—builds on the Triangle Base and creates a large, pointed flap.

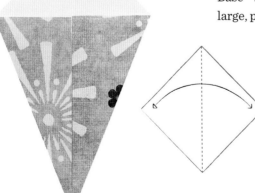

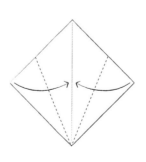

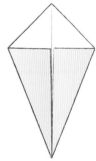

1. Fold in half, left to right. Unfold.

2. Fold both sides to the center, forming a point at the bottom.

FINISHED KITE BASE!

FISH BASE

The Fish Base is a direct extension of the Kite Base. The most popular model made from this base is the traditional whale.

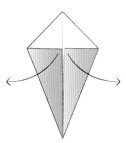

1. Start with the Kite Base. Unfold.

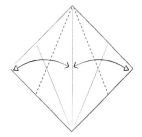

2. Fold both sides to the center, forming a point at the top. Unfold.

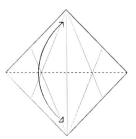

3. Fold in half, bottom to top. Unfold.

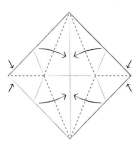

4.a Pinch the left and right sides and collapse to the center along the diagonal fold lines. Fold the flaps up.

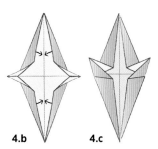

4.b   **4.c**

FINISHED FISH BASE!

CUPBOARD BASE

This is a simple base that is the foundation of several traditional models. It has a fitting name since you fold the sides in like cupboard doors.

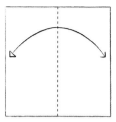

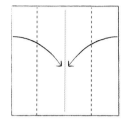

1. Fold in half, left to right. Unfold.

2. Fold both sides to the center.

FINISHED CUPBOARD BASE!

BLINTZ BASE

The person who coined this term mistook a blintz for a knish—a pastry where the four corners are folded into the center. But despite the mistake, the term stuck, and now we have a Blintz Base in origami! In Japan this is called the Cushion Base, since making cushions also involves bringing the four corners into the center.

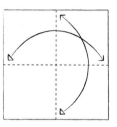

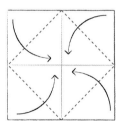

1. Fold in half, edge to edge, in both directions. Unfold.

2. Fold all 4 corners to the center.

FINISHED BLINTZ BASE!

PIG BASE

This base is very versatile because it gives you six flaps (three on each side). Variations on this form are often used to create animals with four legs—the remaining two flaps are used to create the head and tail.

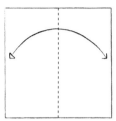

1. Fold in half, left to right. Unfold.

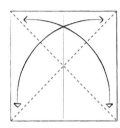

2. Fold in half, corner to corner, in both directions. Unfold.

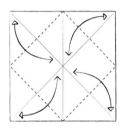

3. Fold all 4 corners to the center. Unfold. Flip over.

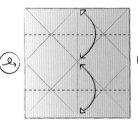

4. Fold the top and bottom to the center. Unfold. Flip over.

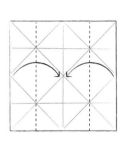

5. Fold both sides to the center.

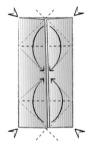

6.a Push in on all 4 corners until the flaps meet at the center.

6.b

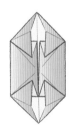

6.c

FINISHED PIG BASE!

WINDMILL BASE

The Windmill Base starts out very similar to the Pig Base—oftentimes it is categorized as the same base! However, I consider it a separate base because some of the folds made to collapse it in the end are different.

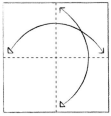

1. Fold in half, edge to edge, in both directions. Unfold.

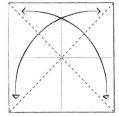

2. Fold in half, corner to corner, in both directions. Unfold. Flip over.

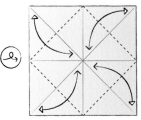

3. Fold all 4 corners to the center. Unfold. Flip over.

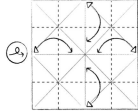

4. Fold all 4 edges to the center. Unfold.

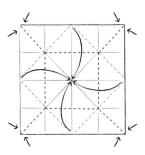

5.a Pinch all 4 corners while collapsing the edges to the center.

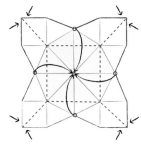

5.b

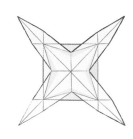

5.c

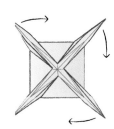

6. Fold the flaps to the left.

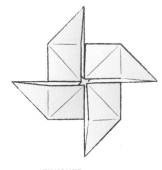

FINISHED WINDMILL BASE!

PRELIMINARY BASE

This is the base of bases. It's the start of the Bird Base and the Frog Base, and there are many amazing models that start from it too. The Preliminary Base is essentially the complete reverse of the Waterbomb Base.

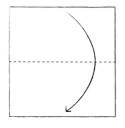

1. Fold in half, top to bottom.

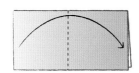

2. Fold in half, left to right.

3. On the front layer, fold the top right corner down.

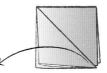

4. Open the front flap to the left (keep the triangle folded).

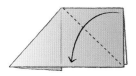

5. Fold the top right corner down.

6.a Open the pocket at the bottom and then collapse so that the left and right sides meet.

Note: *Make sure to open up the big pocket and not the pocket of one of the triangles. Your result should be a square with 4 points on the bottom.*

6.b

6.c

FINISHED PRELIMINARY BASE!

BIRD BASE

The paper crane is probably the most easily recognized origami model. The crane—and many other origami birds—all start from the appropriately named Bird Base.

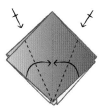

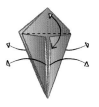

1. Start with the Preliminary Base, (page 31) closed corner at the top. On the front layer, fold both sides to the center, forming a point at the bottom. Repeat on the other side.

2. Fold the top down. Unfold back to the Preliminary Base.

3. Fold the top down along the existing crease.

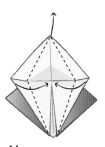

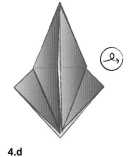

4.a Open the front layer, bringing the bottom corner upward while holding down the other layers. Collapse along the fold lines. Flip over.

Note: *Keep the top triangle folded during the early part of this step. It helps reverse the folds on the front layer, and the sides will start to collapse toward the center.*

4.b

4.c

4.d

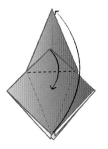

5. Fold the top triangle down along the existing crease. Repeat step 4.

FINISHED BIRD BASE!

FROG BASE

This classic base is the hybrid of many of the previous bases. It seems complicated at first, but once you fold it a few times the repetitive sequences will become second nature.

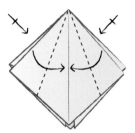

1. Start with the Preliminary Base, (page 31). On the front layer, fold both sides to the center, forming a point at the top. Repeat on the other side.

2. Unfold back to the Preliminary Base.

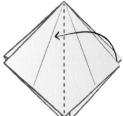

3. On the front layer, fold the right side upward until it is perpendicular to the base.

Note: *The model will momentarily be 3D until you finish step 4.*

4.a Open the pocket of the perpendicular piece and squash fold using the existing fold lines.

Note: *You will need to reverse one crease to squash fold in this step.*

4.b

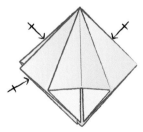

5. Repeat steps 3 and 4 on the remaining 3 flaps.

FINISHED FROG BASE!

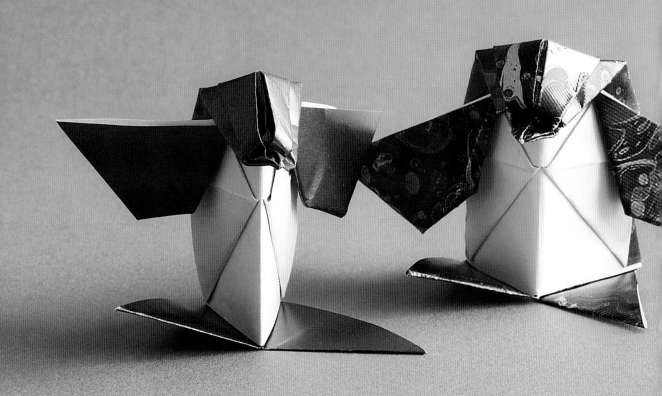

Small

I love creating origami animals and creatures with steps that flow smoothly from start to finish. Easy-to-spot folding landmarks and a clear order of events—both visual and narrative—help make a new project enjoyable from the first try. But for me, one of the most appealing aspects to a pint-sized origami creation is the "wow" moment when the tiny paper animal suddenly springs to life with the final fold. Hopefully, the following designs will not only seem intuitive and easy to follow, but also lead to some of these "wow" moments for you, too! I hope you have as much fun folding these new friends as I did designing them.

Songbird

The traditional dove is a classic origami model. My variation is flatter and more expressive, thanks to simple adjustments to the angles and placement of the folds. I think of it as a songbird because of the words that originally went with it on the greeting card I designed: "Sing a song of joy, sing a song of happiness, just sing." It is just a coincidence that my last name happens to be Song!

Paper Information I used a 6″ (15cm) square of paper to make a bird that measures about 4″ (10cm). Out of the two shown here, I prefer the solid color, which really brings out the elegance in the model.

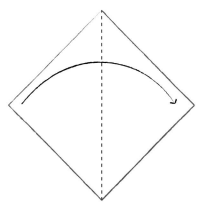

1. Fold in half, left to right.

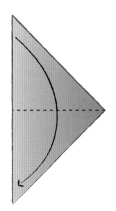

2. Fold in half, top to bottom.

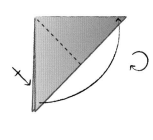

3. Fold the front flap up. Repeat on the other side. Rotate.

4. On the front layer, fold the bottom corner to the top. Unfold.

5.a On the front layer, inside reverse fold the bottom corner.

5.b

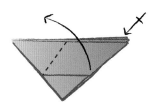

6. Fold the right corner up to create the wing. Repeat steps 3–6 on the other side.

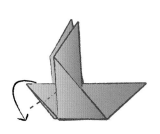

7. Inside reverse fold the left corner to create the head and beak.

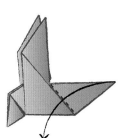

8. Fold the right corner down to create the tail.

9. Open and squash fold the tail.

FINISHED SONGBIRD!

Swimming Turtle

This playful turtle was designed for my line of Creased, Inc., greeting cards. I was looking for a simple model that was flat but very representational so that everyone would know exactly what they were looking at when they pulled the card out of the envelope!

Paper Information Using a 6″ (15cm) square of paper is great for this model. To make it look more like a real turtle, try to find papers with a grid or a print (like tortoiseshell).

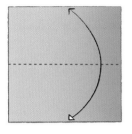

1. Fold in half, bottom to top. Unfold.

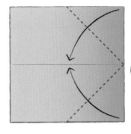

2. Fold the right corners to the center. Flip over.

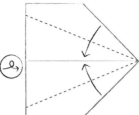

3. Fold the right edges to the center.

Note: *The triangle flaps will flip out from behind.*

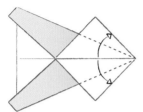

4. Fold the right edges to the center. Unfold.

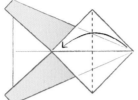

5. Fold the right corner of the square to the left corner.

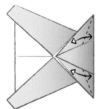

6. On the front layer, fold the top and bottom corners to meet the diagonal crease. Unfold.

Note: *Don't fold too far or step 8 will be very hard!*

7. On the front layer, fold the left corner to the right.

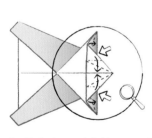

8.a Swivel squash fold using the existing creases to shape the head and front feet.

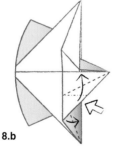

8.b

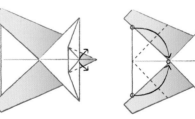

9. On the front layer, fold the flaps out to finish the head.

10. Fold the left edges to the center.

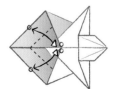

11. On the front layer, fold the flaps left. Unfold.

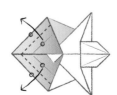

12. On the front layer, fold the flaps left, lining up the previous creases with the edges.

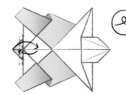

13. Fold the left corner to the right and then back to the left, but shorter than before, to create a pleat for the tail. Flip over.

FINISHED SWIMMING TURTLE!

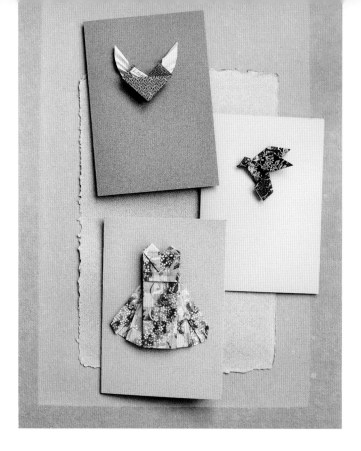

ORIGAMI GREETING CARDS

Greeting cards are a passion of mine, and since origami lends itself so nicely to custom cards, they are also one of my favorite things to make.

My company, Creased, Inc., was founded on the concept of making simple yet elegant origami greeting cards. It has been honored by the trade magazine *Greetings etc.* and won a LOUIE Award (the International Greeting Card Award). Winning the award was amazing, but half the fun is feeling the inspiration from all the beautiful cards nominated for the awards!

You can use many of the origami models in this book to create your own handmade cards. I have used some of them myself! To start, just buy a few blank greeting cards. These are readily available at art supply and stationery stores and often come with matching envelopes.

You can also make your own blank cards. The standard size for cards is 5" × 7" (12.5cm × 18cm), and invitations are generally 4 ½" × 5" (11.5cm × 12.5cm). The standard weight for card stock is 70 lb (184gms), but this will vary depending on the paper and texture you use. The choice of paper for your card can help it make the leap from ho-hum to elegant.

Next all you have to do is select, fold, and attach your favorite origami model with glue. Try to choose a model that lies flat. As for size, I often fold models from squares that are no bigger than 4" (10cm) to use on a greeting card or 3" (7.5cm) for a smaller invitation. If you're using special paper to make the origami, test the size with scrap paper before folding the final model. If you're planning to place more than one model on a card, the size of each model should be even smaller.

T. T. the Rooster

I run an origami club that meets
once a month in New York City.
One of the assistant organizers,
Tricia Tait, is a talented creator of
origami jewelry. Since the Rooster
is her Chinese zodiac symbol
and she collects various rooster,
hen, and chicken ornaments,
I named this bird for her.

Paper Information   If you want to make a rooster, I think it is best if you use paper with red on one side and white on the other side. I used a 6″ (15cm) square, which made a rooster that measured about 3″ (7.5cm).

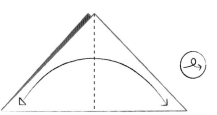

1. Start with the Triangle Base (page 25), white side out. Fold in half, left to right. Unfold. Flip over.

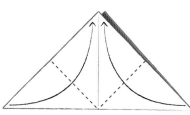

2. Fold both bottom corners to the top.

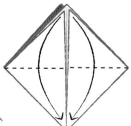

3. On the front layer, fold the top corners to the bottom.

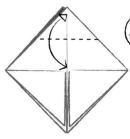

4. Fold the top corner of the remaining layers to the center crease. Unfold only the front layer. Flip over.

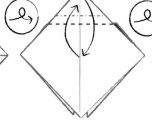

5. Fold the top corner down and then back up again, but shorter than before, to create a pleat. Flip over.

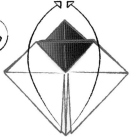

6. On the front layer, unfold the bottom flaps.

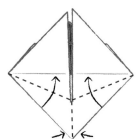

7.a Rabbit ear fold the bottom half of the model.

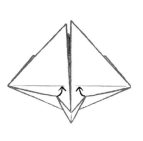

7.b

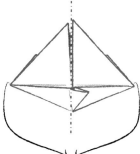

8.a Mountain fold in half through the center.

Note: *In origami a step like this is referred to as "downward chicken."*

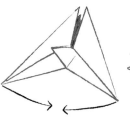

8.b

8.c

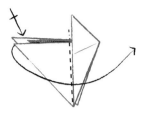 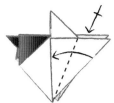  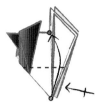

9. On the front layer, fold the left flap right along the existing crease. Repeat on the other side.

10. On the front layer, fold the left flap right to meet the existing crease. Repeat on the other side.

11. Holding the back of the model firmly, pinch the back of the head and pull it upward.

12. On the front layer, fold the bottom corner to the top of the body. Repeat on the other side.

FINISHED T. T. THE ROOSTER!

LMNO Polar Bear

Marcio Noguchi is the technical editor for this book and an amazing guy who has time and again offered his valuable folding expertise. He also bears a unique nickname, "LMNO," which made me want to name this bear for him!

Paper Information   Folding the bear with all white or light blue and white paper makes it immediately recognizable as a polar bear, but you can use brown or black paper for a grizzly or other type of bear. The one shown here was folded from 6″ (15cm) paper.

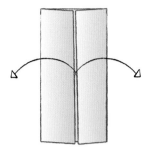

1. Start with the Cupboard Base (page 28), white side out. Unfold back to a square.

2. Fold the right side to the nearest crease.

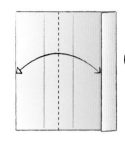

3. Fold the left side to the rightmost crease. Unfold. Flip over.

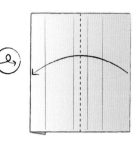

4. Fold in half, right to left.

5. On the front layer, fold the left corners to the edge.

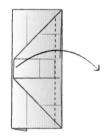

6.a Fold the flap along the rightmost existing crease. Flip over.

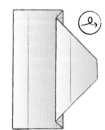

6.b

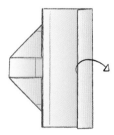

7. Unfold the rectangle flap.

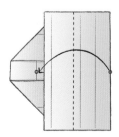

8. Fold the right edge to the leftmost crease.

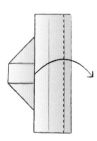

9. On the front layer, fold the left edge along the rightmost crease.

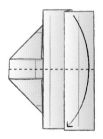

10. Fold in half, top to bottom.

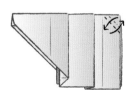

11. Fold the top right corner down and then back up again, but shorter than before, to create a pleat. Unfold.

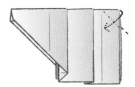 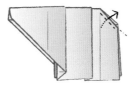 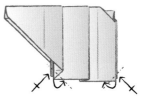 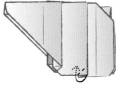

12. Inside reverse fold the top right corner to the first crease line to start the tail.

13. Inside reverse fold again along the second crease line to finish the tail.

14. Mountain fold the bottom left and right corners. Repeat on the other side.

15. Fold the corner of the center flap. Unfold.

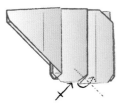 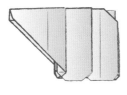

16. Inside reverse the corner of the center flap to finish separating the legs. Repeat steps 15–16 on the other side.

FINISHED LMNO POLAR BEAR!

Lucky Frog

I designed this frog while collaborating with an award-winning accessory designer on origami-inspired hats and bags. Like frogs everywhere, it's a symbol of good fortune. But if you want your frog to be lucky, you have to give it to someone else! You pass the luck on and it will hop back to you— it's true origami karma.

Paper Information There are a lot of colors and textures of paper that make great frogs. I think that a 6″ (15cm) square is a good size to start with, but once you make one you should challenge yourself to fold smaller and smaller if you can!

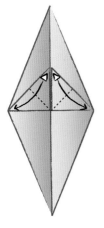

1. Start with the Fish Base (page 27). On the front layer, fold the top corners of the flaps to the edges. Unfold.

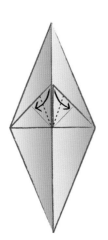

2. On the front layer, fold the top corners of the flaps to the previous creases. Flip over.

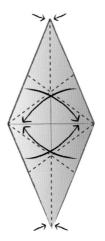

3.a Rabbit Ear Fold the top and bottom. Pinch the tips and collapse.

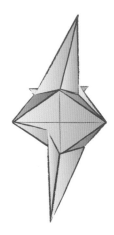

3.b

3.c

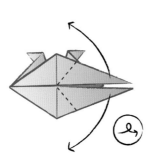

4. Fold the right side flaps out. Flip over.

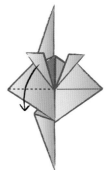

5. Fold the left flap down.

6. Fold the left corner to the right corner.

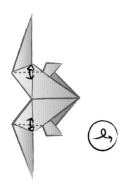

7. Fold the corners of the body in. Unfold. Flip over.

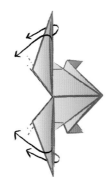

8.a Outside reverse fold the flaps to create the legs.

Note: *There are no new creases—just be gentle and this should happen easily.*

8.b

9. Fold the flaps from step 7 underneath the model.

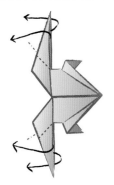

10. Outside reverse fold part of the legs.

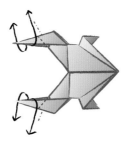

11. Outside reverse fold the legs along the previous creases to create feet.

12. On the front layer, fold the flaps outward.

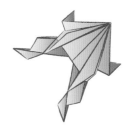

FINISHED LUCKY FROG!

LEATHER AND SNAKESKIN FOLDING

I first experimented with folding snakeskin and leather as part of an accessories design course. With leather you're limited to simple folds because of the thickness of the material, but some people find it works well for geometric patterns and other simple shapes to create texture. With snakeskin you're limited to the size of the skin, but as you can see on page 47, the effect it has can lead to a wonderful piece of origami!

Alan the Bunny

The inspiration for this cute bunny came from a children's book my friend Alan is writing about the adventures of a baby rabbit and his mother. The final steps of this model use a nontraditional method of rounding out the back—folds and friction create the tension the model needs to form the tail. It's tricky at first, but once you get the hang of it you will be able to reproduce these as fast as real bunnies!

Paper Information   Paper that is 6″ (15cm) square will create a 3″ (7.5cm) bunny with very long ears. For this guy, don't use paper that is too stiff or thick because it will make the final fold more difficult.

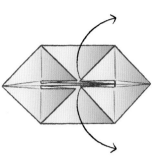

1. Start with the Pig Base (page 29). Pinch the corners of the flaps on the right side and pull outward.

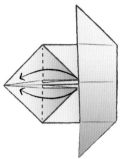

2. On the front layer, fold the flaps to left.

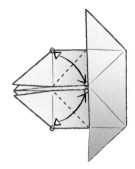

3. Fold. Unfold.

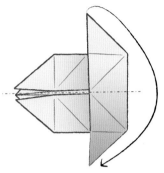

4. Mountain fold in half, top to bottom.

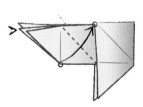

5.a Pinch the left corner inside the flaps and push downward while brining the front and back layers upward.

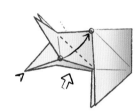

5.b

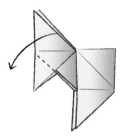

6. On the front layer, fold the top right edge of the triangle to the bottom left corner to start the ear.

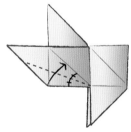

7. Fold the bottom of the ear to the existing crease.

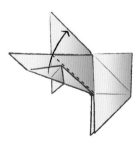

8. Fold the ear to the right.

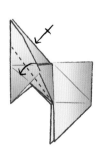

9. Fold the right edge of the ear to the left. Repeat steps 6–9 on the other side.

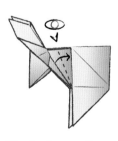

10.a Gently open the top and fold the ears to the center.

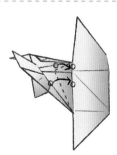

10.b

11. Fold the bottom corner up to start the leg.

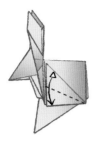

12. Fold the front flap in half, top to bottom. Unfold.

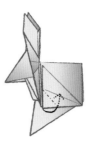

13. Mountain fold the bottom left corner.

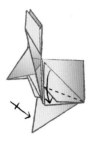

14. Fold the top right edge of the front flap to the bottom. Repeat steps 11–14 on the other side.

15. Fold the left corner up to create the nose.

16. Fold the top right corner to the bottom and then fold back up, but shorter than before, to pleat. Unfold.

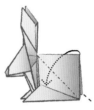

17. Inside reverse fold the top right corner along the leftmost crease.

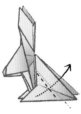

18. Inside reverse fold again along rightmost crease to create the tail.

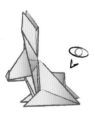

19.a View your model from the back; bring the bottom corners together. ***Note:*** *See page 9 for a photo that shows how the legs lock together.*

19.b

20. Bring feet forward to finish.

FINISHED ALAN THE BUNNY!

ORIGAMI JEWELRY

Showcase your origami by making an origami brooch or a pair of earrings! Origami jewelry is easy to make and a fun way to accessorize. Almost any origami model could work if made in miniature. However, choosing the right size paper for a particular model is important. Remember, different models that start with the same size of paper can end up different finished sizes.

To make a decorative pin, use either a self-adhesive pin back or affix the origami to a pin back with super glue or hot glue (sewing isn't practical, as the paper might rip). For earrings, you can use the origami with many different types of findings that are available for jewelry making. You can use it with beads to add weight or jump rings to add length. Simply poke a hole in the origami and work an eye pin, ear wire, or jump ring through it, and you can attach the origami to the earring wire of your choice. All jewelry-making supplies can be found at your local craft or bead store.

Your origami jewelry will require some sort of protective coating so it can withstand regular wear and use. Tricia Tait, of T8 Studios, recommends sealing the paper with a fixative and then coating the finished model multiple times with an acrylic coating. The result is a brilliant, shiny surface with durable protection that makes the jewelry long lasting. In a pinch, you can also use clear nail polish to protect your pieces.

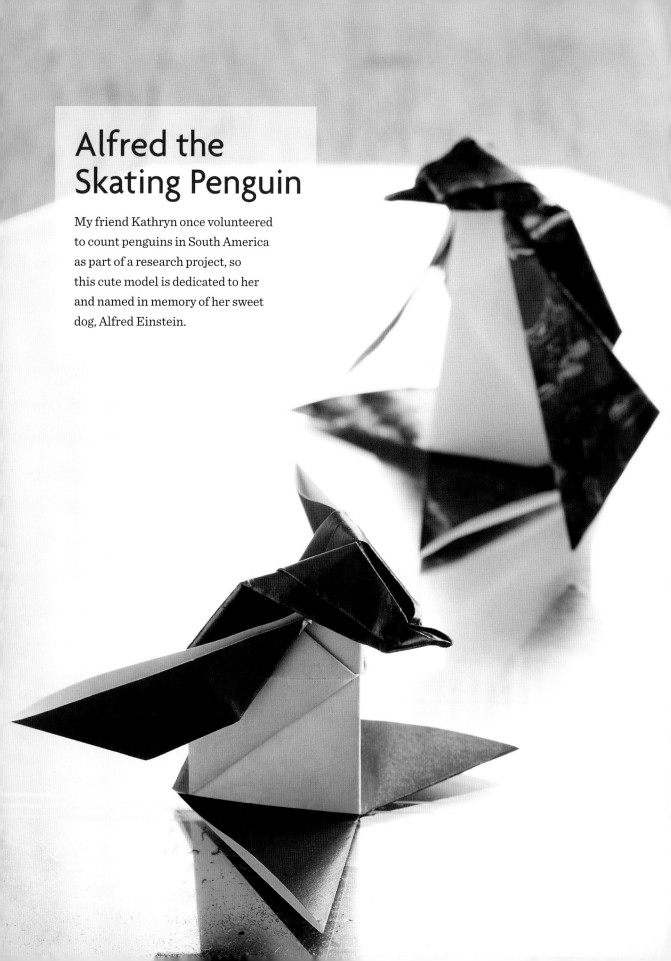

Alfred the Skating Penguin

My friend Kathryn once volunteered to count penguins in South America as part of a research project, so this cute model is dedicated to her and named in memory of her sweet dog, Alfred Einstein.

Paper Information This model uses both sides of the paper, so it is a great model for any two-sided paper you might have handy. A 6″ (15cm) square will shrink down to a 3″ (7.5cm) penguin, so you may want to fold from a larger sheet to make detailed shaping easier.

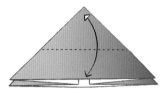

1. Start with the Waterbomb Base (page 26). Fold the top corner to the bottom. Unfold.

2. Fold the top corner to the existing crease. Unfold.

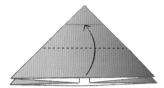

3. Fold the bottom to the crease from step 2.

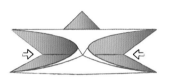

4.a Open the front flap and squash fold the color pockets. Flip over.

Note: *When you squash fold, make sure to line up the edges and make a flat square in the center.*

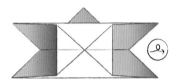

4.b

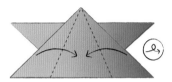

5. On the front layer, fold both sides to the center. Flip over.

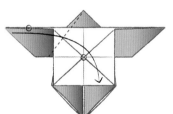

6. Fold the left flap over the intersection of the existing creases.

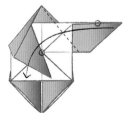

7. Fold the right flap over the intersection of the existing creases.

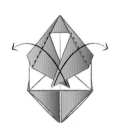

8. Fold the flaps back out, with the bottom edges lining up to the center fold of the body to create wings.

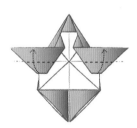

9. Inside reverse fold the bottom of the wings.

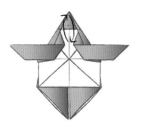   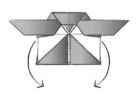

10. Fold the top corner down and then back up, but shorter than before, to pleat.

11. Fold the bottom flaps up.

12. Fold the top down to create the head.

13. Mountain fold in half, left to right.

14. Open the legs and shape the head by pulling it up slightly.

FINISHED ALFRED THE SKATING PENGUIN!

ACTION MODELS

This is a very playful penguin! It is an example of what's called an "action model," which means that the design has a feature that makes it easy to move or play with in some way. In this case, when you put the penguin on a smooth surface and blow on it, the large feet will help him keep his balance and skate across the table!

Sok-a-Roo
the Baby Kangaroo

Just like any group of friends, my lunch buddies and
I all have nicknames for each other. Since my friend
Berna calls me Sok-a-Loo, I named this little guy
Sok-a-Roo! The beautiful cave paper you see here
was handmade by Amanda Degener in Minneapolis.

Paper Information The kangaroo you see was folded from a 6″ (15cm) sheet of cave paper, but you can use almost any sturdy stock. A paper with some stiffness will make the shaping easier.

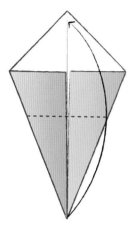

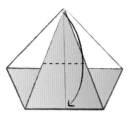

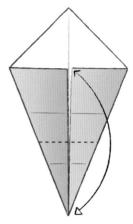

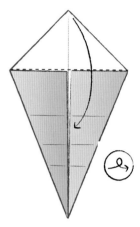

1. Start with the Kite Base (page 26). Fold the bottom corner to the top.

2. On the front layer, fold the top corner to the bottom. Unfold back to Kite Base.

3. Fold the bottom corner to the base of the top triangle. Unfold.

4. Fold the top down along the base of the triangle. Flip over.

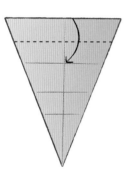

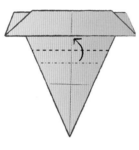

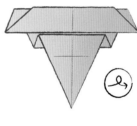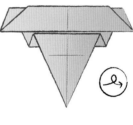

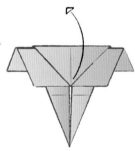

5. Fold the top down to the nearest existing crease.

6.a Fold the existing mountain crease to the edge of the top layer to pleat. Flip over.

6.b

7. Unfold the front layer.

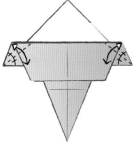

8. Fold the side corners down. Unfold.

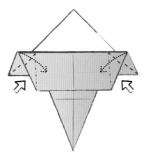

9. Open the front pocket and swivel squash fold the side corners along the existing creases.

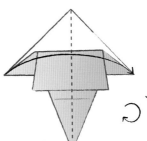

10. Fold in half, left to right. Rotate.

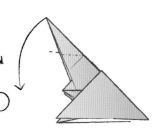

11. Inside reverse fold the top along the existing crease to create the head.

12. Unfold the front layer of the head.

13. Fold the head to the right as far as possible, then fold to the left, but shorter than before, to pleat.

14. Mountain fold the left corner of the head.

15. Fold the head, right to left.

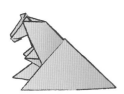

FINISHED SOK-A-ROO THE BABY KANGAROO!

Nemesis Gorilla

This model is dedicated to my dear friend Alexander; we have known each other for a very long time. As our friendship and careers have evolved over the years, we have often felt an underlying competition between us—a friendly one that makes us both try even harder at whatever we are doing. As best friends, we playfully refer to each other as "nemesis," mainly because we are so similar and yet also very different.

Paper Information   The gorilla uses both sides of the paper and shrinks a 6″ (15cm) piece of paper down to about half the original paper size. For a fun twist, try finding some paper with a velvety texture for "fur"!

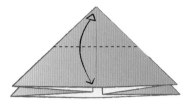

1. Start with the Water-bomb Base (page 26). Fold the top corner to the bottom. Unfold.

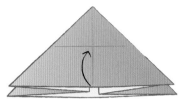

2. Fold the bottom to the existing crease.

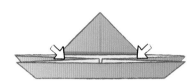

3. Open the flap from inside the 2 side pockets and squash fold along the creases.

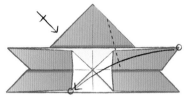

4.a Fold the top right corner of the flap to the bottom left corner of the center square to create an arm. Repeat on the other side. Flip over.

Note: *When you fold the left flap down, the left arm will cross the right.*

4.b

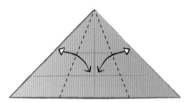

5. Fold the sides to the center. Unfold.

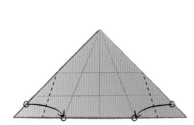

6. Fold the bottom of the sides down.

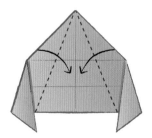

7.a Fold along the creases from step 5. Flip over.

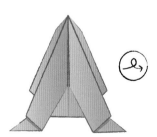

7.b

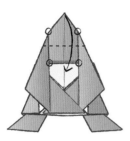

8. Fold the top corner down to create the head.

9. Fold the bottom of the head up, almost to the top.

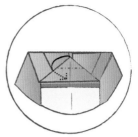

10. Mountain fold the corner of the flap.

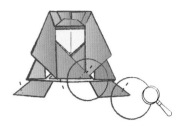

11.a Inside reverse fold the tips of the arms and legs.

11.b

12. Bend the arms forward and up slightly.

FINISHED NEMESIS GORILLA!

Kitty Cat

This adorable model is yet another result of a happy accident after doodling with paper and trying out variations of bases. It uses multiple rabbit ear folds to create flaps that eventually become the legs, body, and tail.

Paper Information Try folding a 6″ (15cm) Kitty Cat with interesting printed wrapping papers or decorative paper. Even if your paper only has a design on one side, this Kitty Cat will still look good.

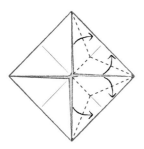 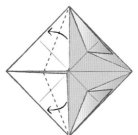 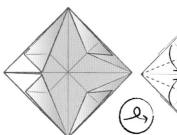 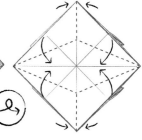

1. Start with the Blintz Base (page 28), white side out. Rabbit ear fold the top right and bottom right.

2.a Fold the left flaps to the edge. Flip over.

2.b

3. Rabbit ear fold the top and bottom.

Note: *The triangles on the side will flip out from underneath.*

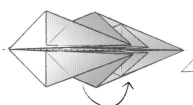 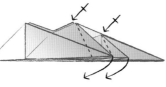 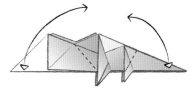

4. Mountain fold, bottom to top.

5. Fold flaps forward to create legs. Repeat on the other side.

6. Fold the left and right sides up. Unfold.

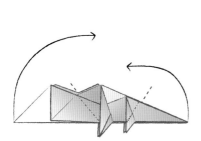 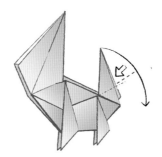 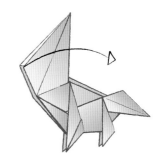

7. Inside reverse fold along the existing creases.

8. Open and squash fold the top right corner to create the tail.

9. Open the top left flap to create the head.

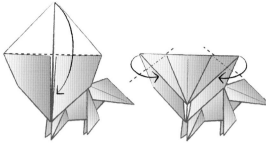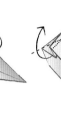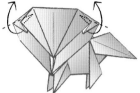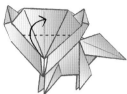

10. Fold the top corner of the head down.

11. Inside reverse fold the top corners of the head.

12. Inside reverse fold the corners again to create the ears.

13. On the front layer of the head, fold the bottom corner up.

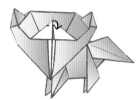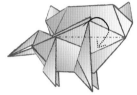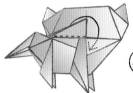

14. On the front layer of the head, fold the top corner down to create the nose. Flip over.

15. Mountain fold the front flap, tucking it behind the head.

16. Fold the remaining flap down, tucking it behind the leg.

FINISHED KITTY CAT!

Kyoko's Swallow

The graceful bird is symbolic of many things, from good fortune and good health to loyalty and love, as well as a token for a safe return home. I first met Kyoko when I taught at an OrigamiUSA Special Folding Fun Session, and whenever I spend time with her and her husband, Shig, I really feel that I've come home to my second family.

Paper Information   This model is very flexible when it comes to paper choice; I've folded it from various sizes and different thicknesses. A 7″ (18cm) square will result in a bird perfect for using in a mobile (see page 106).

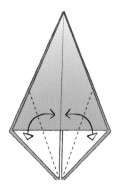

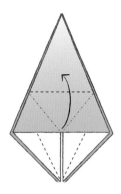

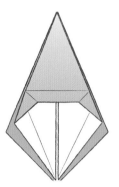

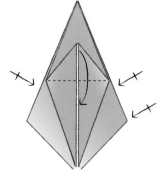

1. Start with the Frog Base (page 33). On the front layer, fold the bottom flaps to the center. Unfold.

2.a On the front layer, fold the bottom edge up, collapsing the left and right sides to the center.

2.b

3. On the front layer, fold the top corner down. Repeat steps 1–3 on the 3 similar sides.

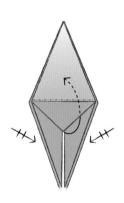

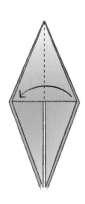

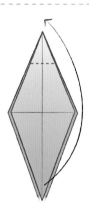

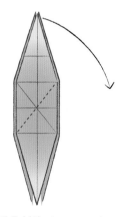

4. Inside reverse fold the bottom triangle flaps of the 4 folded sides. Repeat on left and right sides, not on the back.

Note: *While inside reverse folding, you will tuck the flaps inside and flatten.*

5. On the front layer, fold the right flap to the left.

6. On the front layer, fold the bottom corner all the way up.

7. Fold the top corner to the right along the existing diagonal crease to create a wing.

Note*: This will open up the top layer into a triangle with the wing flap underneath.*

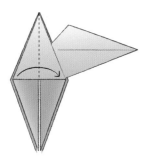
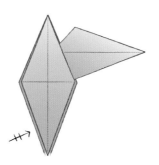
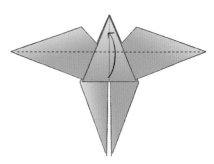

8. On the front layer, fold the left side to the right.

9. Repeat steps 6 and 7, folding the top flap in the opposite direction for the second wing.

10. Fold the wings bottom to top.

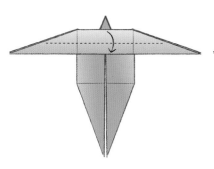
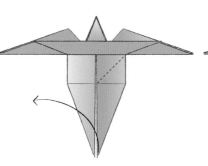
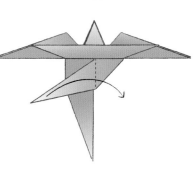

11. On the front layer, fold the wings down.

12. Fold the bottom right flap to the left.

13. Fold the left corner of the same flap to the right.

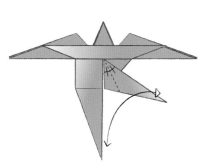
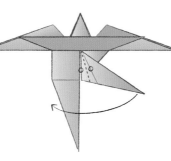
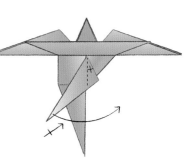

14. Fold the same flap down. Unfold.

15. Fold the same flap to the left, making a new crease between the previous crease and the center.

16. Fold the same flap to the right along the existing crease. Repeat steps 12–16, mirroring the directions, for the bottom left flap.

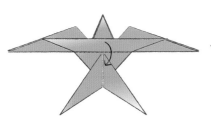

17.a On the front layer, fold the top edge of the wing down. Flip over.

17.b

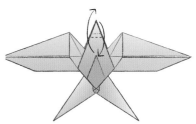

18.a Fold the top corner down, and then back up, but shorter than before, to create a pleat for the beak. Flip over.

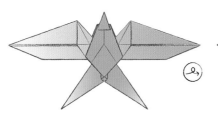

18.b

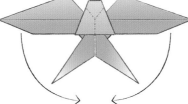

19. Mountain fold the body.

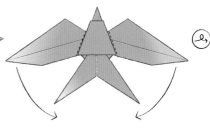

20. Fold the wings along the edge of the body. Flip over.

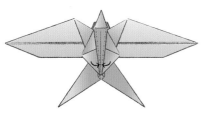

21. Lightly fold body to finish. Flip over.

FINISHED KYOKO'S SWALLOW!

Baby Elephant

Elephants are very popular animals to create and design in the origami world. There are dozens of different types of origami elephants out there, from abstract geometric representations to extremely realistic shapes. My take is on the geometric side, but it is different than most I've seen because of its cute baby form.

Paper Information A 6″ (15cm) square will yield an elephant that stands about 4″ (10cm) tall with the trunk pointing up—which in many cultures is good luck! This is a fun project to fold in larger sizes, too. After you master the folds with standard size paper, turn to page and try making the Momma Elephant!

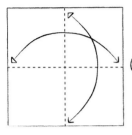 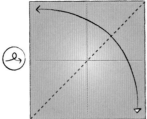 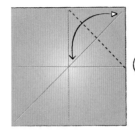

1. Fold in half, edge to edge, in both directions. Unfold. Flip over.

2. Fold the bottom right corner to the top left. Unfold.

3. Fold the top right corner to the center. Unfold. Flip over.

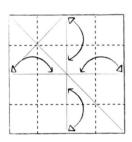 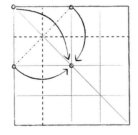 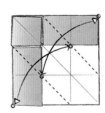 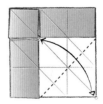

4. Fold all 4 sides to the center. Unfold.

5. Collapse the top corner section (the top left corner will remain on top).

Note: You just formed an "isolated" Preliminary Base (page 31)! Origami animal models often use this isolation technique to create a more distinct separation between the head (or tail) and the body.

6. Fold the top right and bottom left corners to the existing creases. Unfold.

7. Fold the bottom right corner to the Preliminary Base. Unfold.

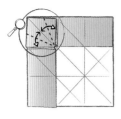 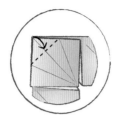 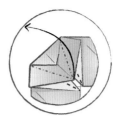 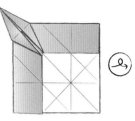

8.a Fold the isolated Preliminary Base into half of a Bird Base (see page 32). Flip over.

8.b

8.c

8.d

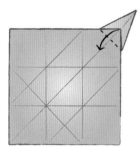 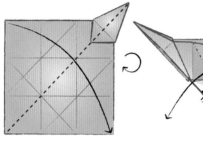 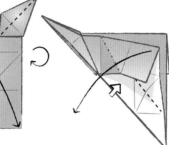 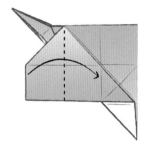

9. On the front layer, fold the top right corner down.

10. Fold in half, top left to bottom right. Rotate.

11. On the front layer, open and squash fold the top right corner.

12. Fold the left edge of the flap right along the existing crease.

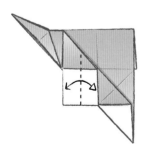 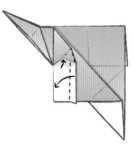 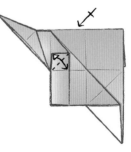 

13. Fold the front layer of the flap. Unfold.

14. Inside reverse fold the flap to create the front leg.

15. Fold the top left corner of the front leg down. Unfold. Repeat steps 11–15 on the other side.

16. Fold the right edge to the existing crease. Unfold.

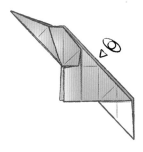

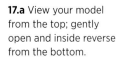

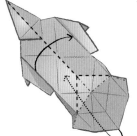

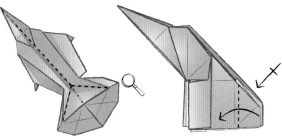

17.a View your model from the top; gently open and inside reverse from the bottom.
Note: *Tuck in the back corner while pinching the sides and closing up the model.*

17.b

17.c

18. Fold the right edge to the left, making the crease slightly to the right of the existing crease. Repeat on the other side.

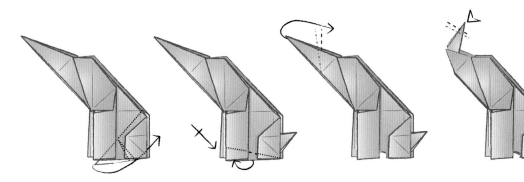

19. Inside reverse fold the flap underneath to create the tail.

20. Tuck in the bottom edge to separate the leg and body. Repeat on other side.

21. Inside reverse fold the left side of the trunk.

22. Inside reverse fold the tip of the trunk.

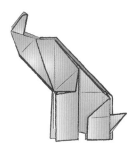

FINISHED BABY ELEPHANT!

Blue Whale

Ever since I visited the Hall of Ocean Life at the American Museum
of Natural History in New York City, I've wanted to design an origami
whale modeled after the giant life-sized one hanging so majestically
in its center. This model uses both sides of the paper to create an
extra dimension. Many origami models utilize a "color change" to add
depth and character.

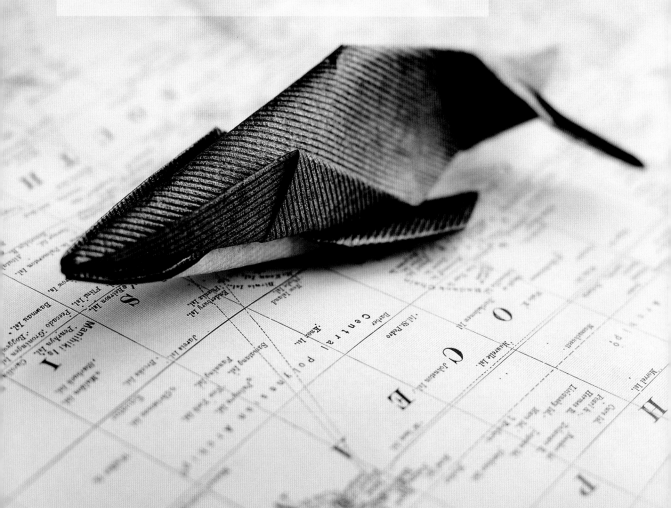

Paper Information This model eats up a lot of paper because of the color change and the fins on the side; you must start with a 10″ (25.5cm) sheet of paper for a finished model just under 5″ (12.5cm).

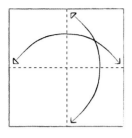

1. Fold in half, edge to edge, in both directions. Unfold.

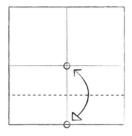

2. Fold the bottom to the center. Unfold.

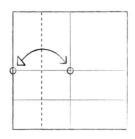

3. Fold the left side to the center. Unfold.

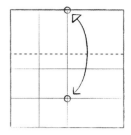

4. Fold the top edge to the bottom crease. Unfold.

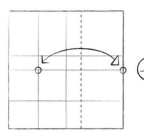

5. Fold the right edge to the leftmost crease. Unfold. Flip over.

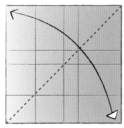

6. Fold the bottom right to the top left. Unfold.

Note: Make sure the diagonals cross through the center of all squares.

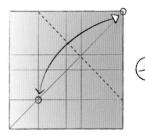

7. Fold the top right down. Unfold. Flip over.

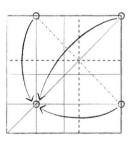

8. Collapse the top right corner as you would a Preliminary Base (page 31).

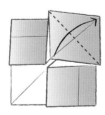

9. On the front layer, fold the bottom left corner to the top right.

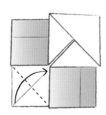

10. Fold the bottom left corner towards the center.

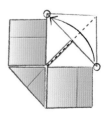

11. On the front layer, fold the bottom right corner to the top left.

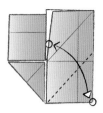

12. Fold the bottom right corner up. Unfold.

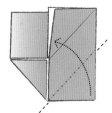

13.a Inside reverse fold the bottom right corner.

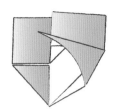

13.b

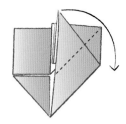

14. Fold the top corner down to the right.

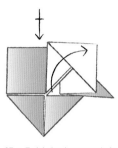

15.a Fold the bottom left corner of square to the upper right. Repeat steps 12–15 on the left side. Rotate.

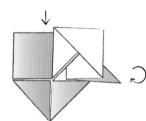

15.b

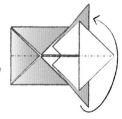

16. Mountain fold the bottom to the top.

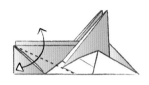

17.a Fold the bottom left corner up. Unfold back to the beginning of step 16 (before mountain fold).

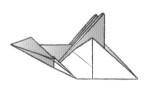

17.b

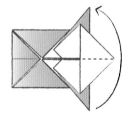

18. Fold the bottom corner to the top.

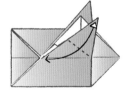

19. On the front layer, fold the top corner down. Unfold.

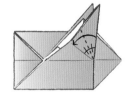

20. On the front layer, fold the top corner to the previous crease to create a fin.

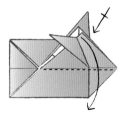

21. On the front layer, fold the top corner down. Repeat steps 18–21 on the top side.

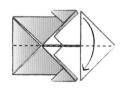

22. Fold the model in half, top to bottom.

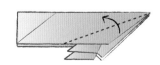

23. On the front layer, fold the bottom right corner up.

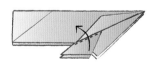

24. Fold the fin up along the edge of body.

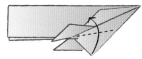

25. On the front layer, fold the bottom flap up.

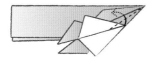

26. On the front layer, fold the right edge to the left and tuck underneath the existing flap.

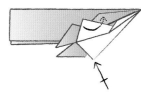

27. Tuck the white flaps underneath the blue flap. Repeat steps 23–27 on the other side.

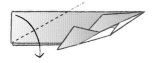

28. Inside reverse fold the left side along the existing creases to create the tail.

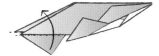

29. Inside reverse fold the tail again.

30. Inside reverse fold the top of the tail to finish.

Note: *Shape the body by pinching the tail and rounding out the front from underneath.*

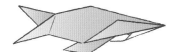

FINISHED BLUE WHALE!

Michael's Butterfly

Michael LaFosse is the virtuoso of origami butterflies and is one of the top American masters of origami. He often names his various beautiful butterfly designs after his friends, so I thought I would name this one for him! This model can be folded with any foreign currency that has the 2:1 ratio.

Paper Information   This butterfly can be done with many different types of currencies. The images shown here are folded from various denominations of Chinese money. You can use any foreign currency or paper whose length is twice the width (2:1).

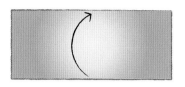

1. Fold in half, bottom to top.

2. Fold in half, left to right. Unfold.

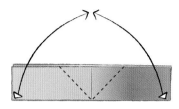

3. Fold the left and right sides up. Unfold.

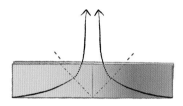

4. Inside reverse fold the sides along the previous creases.

5.a On the front layer, fold the sides to the center. Flip over.

5.b

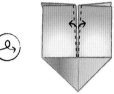

6.a Fold center edges slightly out at an angle. Flip Over

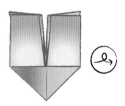

6.b

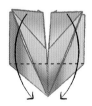

7. Fold top to bottom.

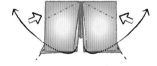

8.a Open and squash fold the sides.

Note: *This is an asymmetrical squash. The extra layer that was in the front will stick out from the bottom. The bottom corners will come to a point but the top corners will not.*

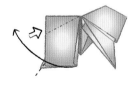

8.b

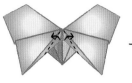 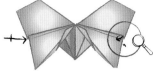 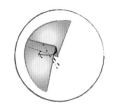 

9. Fold bottom of wings out.

Note: *the bottom corner will need to go past the layer underneath.*

10.a Inside reverse the center flap of the wings.

10.b

10.c. Tucking the flap here underneath will help further separate the wings.

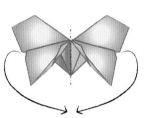 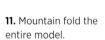  

11. Mountain fold the entire model.

12. Fold the body down, pivoting from the corner.

13. Open the front wing and body along the existing creases.

14. Mountain fold the back wing.

15. Tuck the bottom corners of the body inward to lock. Repeat on the other side.

16. Gently open the wings and center of the body to shape.

FINISHED MICHAEL'S BUTTERFLY!

MONEY FOLDING

When you find yourself without any origami paper, you can always look in your wallet and find a very valuable piece of paper—money! Bill folding has become a popular trend in the origami community. With the rise of new money-folding designers, interest in this subgroup has grown quickly. Won Park from Hawaii is a visionary pioneer: His detailed creations always leave you wondering how the fold is even possible. His online group, Money Folders Unite (see page 156), offers its members diagrams from many creators and folding help too.

As you might expect, origami with money works best when you have crisp, new bills.

You can usually get these at any bank: Sometimes you will have to order them, but often the business counter will have stacks of new bills they would be happy to exchange for you.

Often foreign currency is much more colorful than American money and contains beautiful imagery. However, for the most part they have different proportions than a dollar: The length is twice the width (a ratio of 2:1).

Once you find some models to fold with money, you can use the origami for all sorts of things. It can become a more personal way to give a cash present for a birthday or to leave a tip at your favorite restaurant. Go ahead and get started!

Dollar
Bill Koala

Using the existing print on
money is often a favorite
trick for creators and gives
the final model more impact.
This koala uses the print on a
dollar bill to look more lifelike
than he would otherwise. As
a bonus, this koala also makes
a good finger puppet!

1. Fold the top corners down. Unfold.

2. Fold the top down at the bottom of the existing creases. Unfold. Flip over.

3. Fold the top down halfway between the previous crease and the top. Unfold. Flip over.

4.a Collapse the top square into a Waterbomb Base (page 26) along the existing creases. Flip over.

4.b

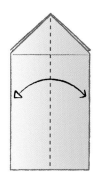

5. On the front layer, fold in half, left to right. Unfold.

6. On the front layer, fold the left and right corners to the center.

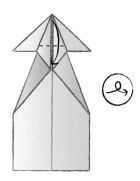

7. Fold the top corner down. Flip over.

Note: *Turning it over and pressing down helps with this fold.*

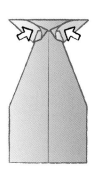

8.a Open and squash fold the top. Flip over.

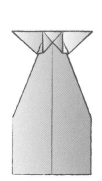

8.b

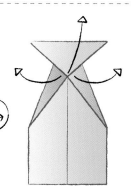

9. Unfold the flaps.

10.a Fold the top left and right corners to the existing crease.

10.b

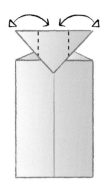

11. Fold the top corners to the center. Unfold.

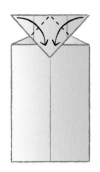

12. Fold the top corners down.

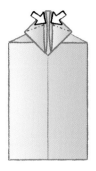

13. Open and squash fold the pockets on the top left and right to create a face.

14. Fold the left and right sides of the face. Unfold.

15. Fold the front layers of the flaps on the face out to the sides.

16. Inside reverse fold the sides of the face.

17. Fold the bottom corner of the face up and then back down again, but shorter than before, to create a pleat for the nose. Flip over.

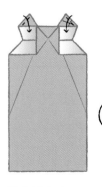

18. Fold the top corners down along the edge. Flip over.

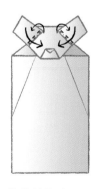

19. Fold the top corners down and then up again, but shorter than before, to create a pleat for the ears.

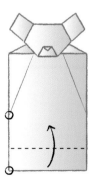

20. Fold the bottom up.

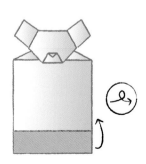

21. Mountain fold the bottom rectangle. Flip over.

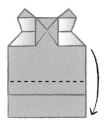

22. Fold the body in half, top to bottom.

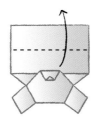

23.a Fold the bottom up. Flip over.

23.b

24. Fold the corners of the body toward the center. Unfold.

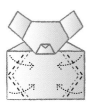

25. Inside reverse fold the corners of the body.

26. Fold the corners of the body lightly to define the arms and legs.

Note: *This fold is more of a blunting of the sides than a true fold.*

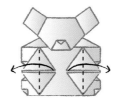

27. Fold the center flaps out.

28. On the top layer, fold the corners toward the center.

29. On the top layer, fold the flaps to the center.

30. Fold the top sides of the body toward the center gently to finish.

Note: *The fold will naturally unfold a bit, and you can then round out the arms and legs.*

FINISHED DOLLAR BILL KOALA!

Medium

Origami isn't just pretty, it can be practical as well. Making boxes, containers, and other functional items is lots of fun and easy to do! In this section, I encourage you to move beyond typical origami paper and experiment with interesting and new materials—reuse old magazines, catalogs, or calendars. There are many fun and beautiful projects you can create just by using a little bit of imagination, and it doesn't have to cost much to be special.

Fabrigami Masu Box

Fabrigami—as you might have guessed—is the folding of fabric to create origami. This fabrigami project uses bookbinding cloth to make a beautiful box. The top and the lid shown here are folded exactly the same way, but the lid is made from a sheet of paper about 5 percent bigger than the base.

Paper Information If you can't find bookbinding cloth, or if you have another piece of fabric you'd rather use, you can back most fabrics with paper using spray adhesive. This box will end up about three-fourths of the original paper size, so it is best to use at least a 10″ (25.5cm) square sheet.

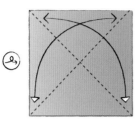

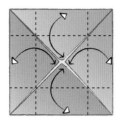

1. Start with the Blintz Base (page 28). Flip over.

2. Fold corner to corner in both directions. Unfold. Flip over.

3. Fold all the sides to the center. Unfold.

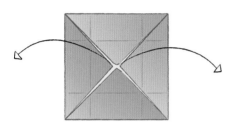

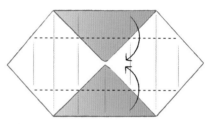

4. Unfold left and right flaps.

5. Fold the bottom and top along the creases so that they are perpendicular to the base.

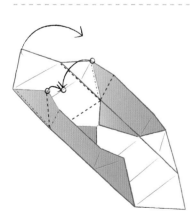

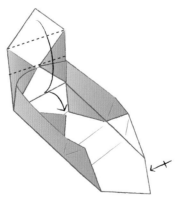

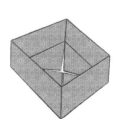

6. Fold the left side perpendicular to the center, collapsing along fold lines.

7. Fold the left side down and in along the creases. Repeat steps 6 and 7 on the right side.

FINISHED FABRIGAMI MASU BOX!

Snack Bowls

These quick and easy-to-make bowls all use rectangular wrap-arounds to lock their shape. If you've already made some of the projects in the Small chapter, this project will help you realize just how versatile some of the traditional bases can be.

Paper Information   You can try folding these bowls from any kind of paper, but the sturdier the better if you're actually going to use them! An 8 ½" (21.5cm) square from a magazine page makes a functional medium-sized bowl, and a 12" (30.5cm) square of scrapbooking paper makes a nice larger-sized bowl.

SNACK BOWL WITH LEGS (PICTURED ON OPPOSITE PAGE, TOP)

 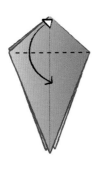 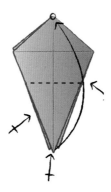 

1. Start with the Bird Base (page 32). Fold the top flaps to the bottom.

2. Fold the top corner down. Unfold.

3. Fold the bottom flap to the top. Repeat steps 2 and 3 on the remaining 3 flaps.

4.a View your model from the bottom; gently open the center, pushing out the corner pockets.

Note: *The flaps you folded will become "trapped" and lock into place as you push the bowl open—the extra paper extends into the legs. The further up you fold the flaps in step 3, the longer the legs will become.*

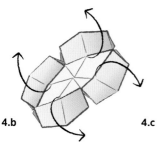 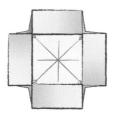 

4.b   **4.c**

FINISHED SNACK BOWL WITH LEGS!

SNACK BOWL (PICTURED ON PAGE 90 AT CENTER)

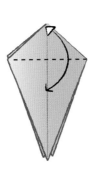 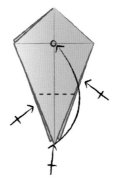 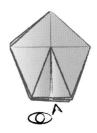

1. Start with the Bird Base (page 32). Fold the top flaps to the bottom.

2. Fold the top corner down. Unfold.

3. Fold the bottom flap to the existing crease. Repeat steps 2 and 3 on the remaining 3 flaps.

4.a View your model from the bottom; gently open the center, pushing out the corner pockets.

Note: *The flaps you folded will become "trapped" and lock into place as you push the bowl open.*

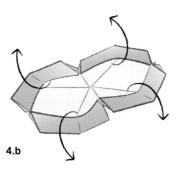

4.b

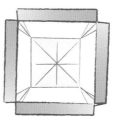

4.c

FINISHED SNACK BOWL!

DELUXE SNACK BOWL (PICTURED ABOVE AND ON PAGE 90, BOTTOM)

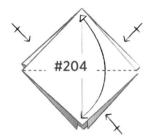

1. Start with the Preliminary Base (page 31), white side out. Fold the top corner to the bottom. Unfold. Repeat on the remaining 3 sides.

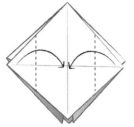

2. On the front layer, fold side corners to the center.

3. On the front layer, open and squash fold the left and right sides.

Note: *This will create 2 isolated partial Frog Bases (see page 33).*

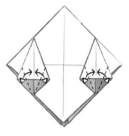

4. Fold the sides of the isolated bases to the center, forming points at the bottoms. Unfold.

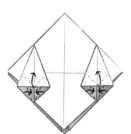

5. Lift up the bottom edge of the isolated bases while collapsing the left and right sides to the center along the existing creases.

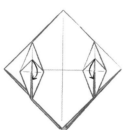

6. On the isolated bases, fold the triangle flaps down.

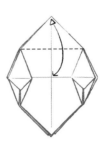

7. Fold the top corner to the center. Unfold.

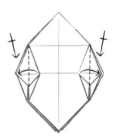

8. On the front layer, fold the interior corners of the isolated bases to the sides. Repeat steps 3–8 on the opposite side.

MEDIUM

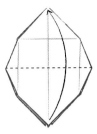

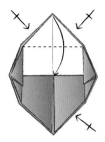

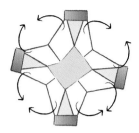

9. On the front layer, fold the bottom to the top.

10. On the front layer, fold the top down to the center. Repeat steps 9–10 on the remaining 3 sides.

11.a View your model from the bottom; gently open the bowl. Pull the pockets out into a rectangle and shape the bottom of the box using the existing creases. ***Note:*** *Be gentle and make sure you don't tear the paper while opening up the triangle points.*

11.b

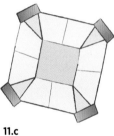

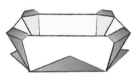

FINISHED DELUXE SNACK BOWL!

11.c

Watercolor Paper Orchid

There are many display options for the orchid
once you have learned to fold the flower.
You can mount them as pictured here using
floral wire and tape. Then simply "plant" them
in a pot using florist foam and add some silk
(or paper!) leaves to replicate a real orchid
arrangement. If the wire wrapping sounds like
too much work, you can buy pre-made stems
at most craft stores and adhere the paper flowers
using a glue gun or glue dots.

Paper Information Watercolor paper comes in many sizes, weights, and textures. For this model, a lighter-weight paper is best. An 8″ (20.5cm) square will make a life-sized orchid.

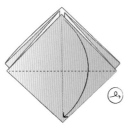 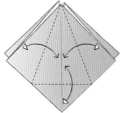 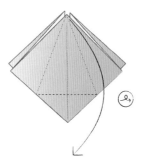

1. Start with the Preliminary Base (page 31). Fold the top corner to the bottom. Flip over.

2.a Fold the sides into the center and the bottom corner up. Unfold.

2.b Open the front layer, bringing the top corner downward while holding down the bottom corner. Collapse along the fold lines. Bring bottom corner up. Flip over.

3. Fold left and right sides to the center. Unfold.

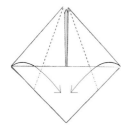 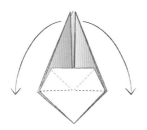 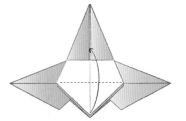

4. Inside reverse fold the sides along the existing creases.

5. Behind the front layer, fold the top flaps down to the sides.

6. On the front layer, fold the bottom corner up as far as possible.

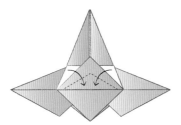 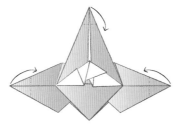 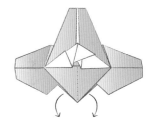

7. Fold the flaps down to create a perpendicular piece in the center.

8. Mountain fold the top and side corners.

9. Mountain fold the bottom triangle to finish.

Note: *Experiment with thinning the petals or folding in the petal corners to make different shapes and variations.*

FINISHED WATERCOLOR PAPER ORCHID!

WET FOLDING

When this model is finished you can paint it with watercolors and add a small amount of shape to the wet paper. This is what is called "wet folding," a process where you dampen the paper to help you shape and mold the model. When paper becomes wet, its fibers expand and change, and it becomes much easier to create curves and gentle shapes. When the paper dries again, it freezes in place and often becomes stronger and stiffer than before. Wet folding is now a popular technique used by many origami artists, such as Ros Joyce and Michael LaFosse.

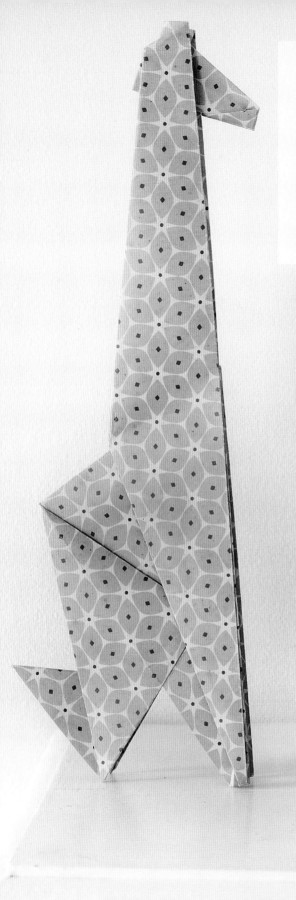

Shivanni the Giraffe

My friend Shivi and I became instant buddies because of our common interest in fashion and all things shiny and glitzy (she used to design for the Nicky Hilton clothing line Chick). Her nickname growing up was Shivanni the Giraffe because of how much taller she was than the other kids, so I decided to name this model after her.

Paper Information The model shown here started with a 12″ (30.5cm) square and yielded a model about 8″ (20.5cm) tall. You can try various decorative or handmade papers, but make sure it is sturdy so the long neck doesn't droop!

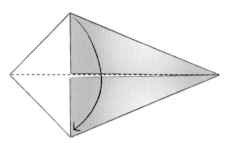

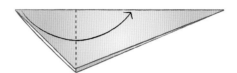

1. Start with the Kite Base (page 26) turned sideways. Fold in half, top to bottom.

2. Fold the left corner to the right.

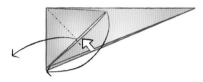

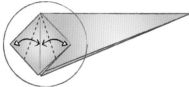

3. Open and squash fold the triangle flap.

4 Fold the left and right edges to the center, forming a sharp point on the top. Unfold.

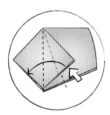

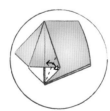

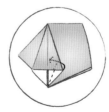

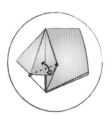

5. Open and squash fold the right side to form a partial Frog Base (see page TK).

6. Fold the bottom right side to the center. Unfold.

7. Inside reverse fold the right side.

Note: *You will fold along the previous crease, but this step will form a new crease too.*

8. Fold the bottom corner up. Unfold.

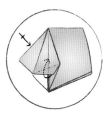

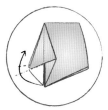

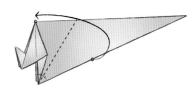

9. Tuck in the bottom along the previous crease. Repeat steps 6–9 on the left side.

10. Inside reverse fold the white triangle to create the tail.

Note: *Use the bottom folded edge as a reference.*

11. Fold the large flap to the left.

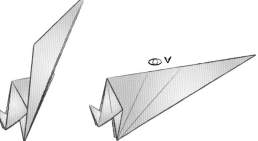

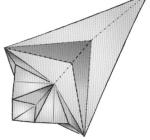

12.a Fold the large flap to the right. Unfold back to the beginning of step 11.

12.b

13.a View your model from the top; outside reverse fold twice, using the existing creases.

13.b

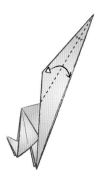

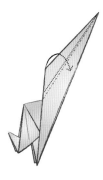

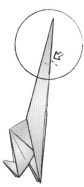

14. Fold the large flap to the right. Unfold.

15. Open and collapse the left side of the large flap along the previous creases.

16. Fold the tip down to the corner of the inside layers. Unfold.

17 Open the top section and squash fold to start the head.

18. Fold the right corner left and then back right again, but shorter than before, to create a pleat.

19. Mountain fold the tip of the right corner to blunt the nose.

20. Fold the head bottom to top.

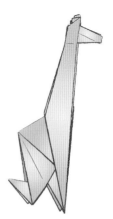

FINISHED SHIVANNI THE GIRAFFE!

Sweetheart Dress

Although this isn't a wearable dress, the shape mimics a free-flowing silhouette with a sweetheart neckline and pleated waist. The design is actually a variation of a napkin fold I designed for an advertising campaign. This version is a little more elegant and slightly more complicated, but it's still doable if you want to try it with a napkin for your next dinner party!

Paper Information   I made the dresses pictured using 12″ (30.5cm) square pieces of scrapbooking paper. This model is also possible with a cloth napkin, although I'd recommend making it without the pleated "belt."

1. Fold left to right, but crease only the very top. Unfold.

2. Using the previous crease as a reference, fold the sides to the center.

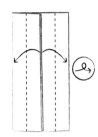

3. Fold the flaps to the edges. Flip over.

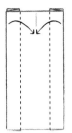

4. Fold the sides to the center. Unfold back to a square.

Note: *The paper is now pleated into eighths.*

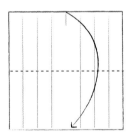

5. Fold top to bottom.

6. On the front layer, fold the bottom edge to the top. Unfold back to a square.

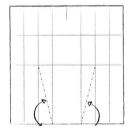

7. Mountain fold, pivoting from the corners of the existing creases. Unfold.

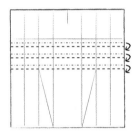

8. Fold and mountain fold the middle of the model to pleat it into eighths.

Note: *Start at the existing center crease with a valley fold and work your way up to the crease above. There will be 6 new folds, as shown.*

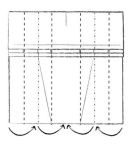  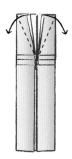 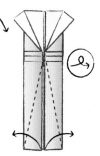

9. Fold sides in along the existing vertical creases.

10. On the front layer, fold the top flaps out slightly to create sleeve cuffs.

11. On the front layer, fold the top flaps out, pivoting from the top of the pleats.

12. On the front layer, fold the bottom flaps out, pivoting from the bottom of the pleats, to create the bottom of the dress. Flip over.

  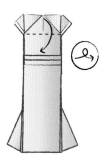 

13. On the front layer, fold the top corners down along the center crease. Unfold.

14. Inside reverse fold the top corners.

15. Fold the top corner down to the top of the pleats. Flip over.

16. Fold the top corners down, tucking them behind the front layer.

17. Fold the top of the sleeves down slightly.

18. Fold the bottom flaps of the dress out along the creases from step 7.

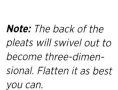

Note: The back of the pleats will swivel out to become three-dimensional. Flatten it as best you can.

19.a Swivel squash fold the corners in the middle of dress so that the sides line up with the bottom of the pleats.

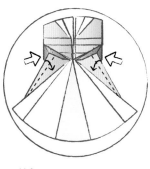

19.b

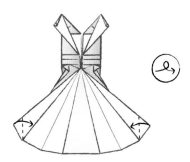

20. Fold the bottom corners toward the center. Flip over.

FINISHED SWEETHEART DRESS!

MOBILES

Origami is great for making mobiles. I've made mobiles out of stars, snowflakes, bubbles, and animals. A simple mobile only requires a couple of things besides paper: some string and Chinese takeout containers. Yes, takeout containers! You won't actually use the containers for the mobile, just the wire handle on the top. The shape is ideal for a mobile, and the loops on the end make it easy to hang your origami models.

To start, string each model through the wire loop after sewing through its center with string or transparent nylon thread. Some models will require two points of attachment—like the head and tail—for better balance. Balancing a

particular hanging model can sometimes take a bit of trial and error, as can finding the balance between the two ends of the wire once they have models attached.

Try moving the strings with the models up and down to find equilibrium. Then, once you find the balance, use a small dab of glue on the string where it meets the wire to keep it there and prevent it from sliding back down. Sometimes adding beads or crystals on the bottom of the models will help to balance them—and also allow them to move and rotate in a more interesting manner. The visual balance of the entire mobile is also important. Try different-sized wires to make your own unique origami mobile.

Message
Heart
with Wings

There are a lot of heart designs
in origami. There are even other
designs for hearts with wings!
This is my version, a simple model
that uses both sides of the paper
to make the wings and the heart
different colors. I did include one
twist: a pocket you can use for a
special message to someone who
makes your heart flutter!

Paper Information   Use paper that has different colors on each side. A 10″ (25.5cm) square was used for the larger heart shown at left, which makes for a great valentine! Of course you can fold it smaller—4″ (10cm) or 5″ (12.5cm)—to affix on a greeting card.

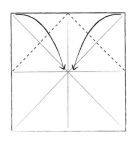

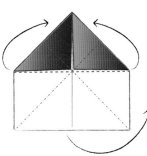

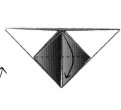

1. Start with the Water-bomb Base (page 26), white side out. Unfold to a square.

2. Fold the top corners to the center.

3. Collapse into a Water-bomb Base, keeping the folds from step 2.

4. On the front layer, fold the top corner to the bottom.

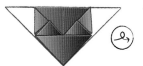

5. Fold the top corners down. Unfold.

6.a Inside reverse fold the top corners. Flip over.

6.b

7. Fold the top to the bottom.

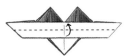

8. On the front layer, fold the left and right sides in.

Note: *This fold should run corner to corner. The edges will not line up with the center triangle (see illustration for step 9).*

9. Fold the bottom edge up.

10. On the front layer, fold in half, bottom to top.

11. Unfold back to the beginning of step 9.

12. On the top flap, pleat the previously folded section into eighths.

Note: *You have already divided the wings into quarters, so this is only 4 new folds. I recommend starting this step with the valley fold on the bottom and working your way up.*

FINISHED MESSAGE HEART WITH WINGS!

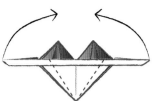

13.a On the front layer, fold the wings up. Flip over.

13.b

Note: *The back layer will fold up, too.*

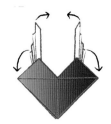

14. Gently open the pleats to expand the wings.

Photo Modular

Chances are you probably have old photographs lying around in boxes. Here is a project to get them out of storage and onto your desk. Folding these simple, modular shapes is easy and fun—and they make great gifts!

Paper Information A modular involves folding multiple pieces of paper and combining them into a larger piece of origami. In this project you'll fold six 4″ x 6″ (10cm x 15cm) photos that will then interlock to create the photo modular shown here, which measures about 5 ½″ x 5 ½″ x 5 ½″ (14cm x 14cm x 14cm). This project also works with 5″ x 7″ photos, business cards, transit cards, and postcards.

PHOTO UNIT (MAKE 6)

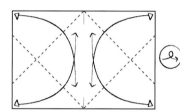

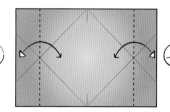

1. Fold in half, left to right, creasing only an inch (2.5cm) of the top and bottom. Unfold.

2. Fold the top and bottom corners in using the previous creases as a guide. Unfold. Flip over.

3. Fold the sides toward the center. Unfold. Flip over.

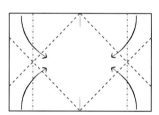

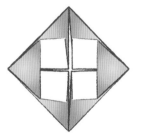

4. Collapse the sides along the existing creases.

Note: *This step is similar to the collapse you learned for the Waterbomb Base (page 26).*

FINISHED PHOTO UNIT!

Note: *Make 5 more units before starting assembly.*

PHOTO MODULAR ASSEMBLY

1.a Insert pointed corners (top and bottom above) into pocketed corners (left and right above) according to the diagram on the following page.

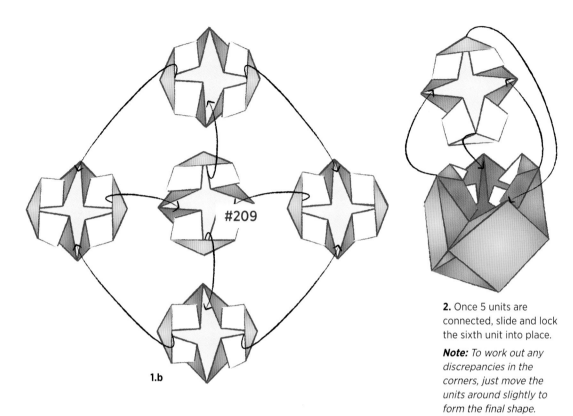

#209

1.b

2. Once 5 units are connected, slide and lock the sixth unit into place.

Note: *To work out any discrepancies in the corners, just move the units around slightly to form the final shape.*

MODULAR ORIGAMI

Modular origami is a type of folding that involves making the same unit multiple times to join together without using any glue. People have come up with all sorts of shapes and often use not only photos but other scrapbooking materials like postcards. The modular stays together thanks to a paper "lock"—the paper squares interlock with each other so the piece doesn't unfold or come apart. When you build a modular, the final piece is the most difficult one to put in, but with practice it will get easier.

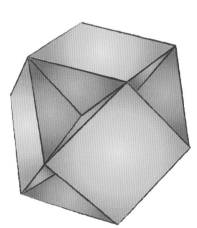

FINISHED PHOTO MODULAR!

Junk Mail Bracelet

Some of you might be familiar with this fold if you spent your school days folding gum wrappers. But did you know you can use any paper to make these folded chains—colorful catalogs, shiny flyers, take-out menus, and other junk mail are all awesome raw materials for this project. I'll show you how to weave together this schoolyard classic for a new custom-made bracelet!

Paper Information   For a regular-sized bracelet it is best to start with small strips, approximately 1 ½"
x 3 ¼" (3.8cm x 8.5cm). For a wider bracelet, 3" x 6 ¼" (7.5cm x 16cm) works
well. The size of the strips used to weave the units together will depend on how
many units you want to link. Just remember to make the weaving strips long
enough to go through all of the chains and still have some length left to fold
back on itself and lock.

JUNK-MAIL BRACELET UNIT (MAKE ABOUT 15-20 FOR ONE CHAIN)

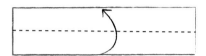

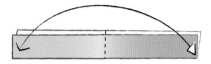

1. Fold in half, bottom
to top.

2. Fold in half, left to
right. Unfold.

3. Fold the left and right
sides toward the center.

*Note: These folds should
not meet the center.*

4. Fold in half, left
to right.

**FINISHED JUNK-MAIL
BRACELET UNIT!**

*Note: Make about 14–
19 more units before
starting assembly*

JUNK-MAIL BRACELET ASSEMBLY

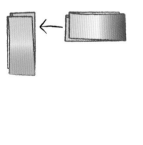

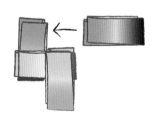

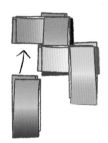

1. Slide one finished unit
into another, making sure
to insert the edges of the
second unit through the
pockets of the first unit.

2.a Repeat the process
until you have your
desired length.

2.b

2.c

3. For single chain bracelet, slide a long strip of paper through the pocket at end of chain. Wrap the chain around and insert the paper through the pocket at the other end. Fold strip on itself and insert it back through any pocket to lock the chain.

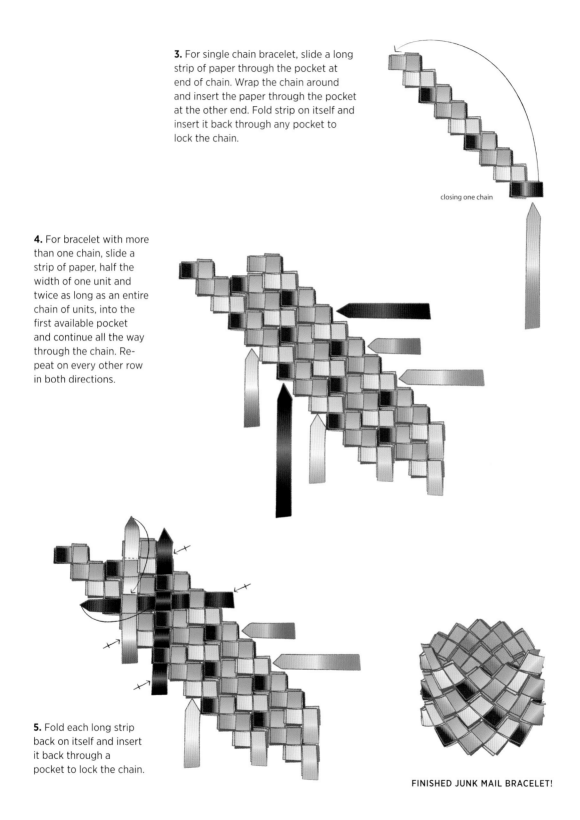

closing one chain

4. For bracelet with more than one chain, slide a strip of paper, half the width of one unit and twice as long as an entire chain of units, into the first available pocket and continue all the way through the chain. Repeat on every other row in both directions.

5. Fold each long strip back on itself and insert it back through a pocket to lock the chain.

FINISHED JUNK MAIL BRACELET!

THE ORIGAMI TREE

For the past several years I have worked on the OrigamiUSA Holiday Tree at New York City's American Museum of Natural History. There is a lot of work involved in creating such a large origami tree, but it is also a fun experience and very rewarding.

A great deal of thought and time goes into choosing the right papers for the museum tree. We've found over the years that dark colors tend to get lost, as do any greens that match the tree. Textured papers are usually nice, but printed papers with busy decorations are not ideal unless the print contributes to the theme of the model. We tend to choose papers with solid colors, visible fibers, and/or a nice sheen. Foil and kami do have their place, but you run the risk of having pieces look either too bland or too crinkled.

Lighting is a key component as well. If you're doing an all origami tree, I would suggest that you don't use internal lights at all. Lights coming from inside the tree can be distracting, and people won't be able to see all the hard work you've put into folding for the tree! Spotlighting is what I'd recommend, and it can be found at any lighting store or most local hardware stores. It really does make a difference.

Before installation, each model has to be checked for "quality assurance" to make sure it's folded well enough to last the entire duration that the tree is displayed. We use green flocked wire inside the models at strategic places so they can be attached to the tree with no wires showing. The models that are hung need to be strung, and mobiles need to be constructed and balanced to hang on the hooks that extend from the tree branches.

Once the tree comes down, models that can be used again are individually packed in tissue paper and stored for another year. It has been a tradition to reuse previous years' models on the tree every year so there is a mix of old and new.

If you want to make your own origami tree ornaments, there are many possibilities. Almost all of the models in this book can be turned into an ornament just by adhering a bit of string to the back. On the following pages are a couple projects that are designed for making ornaments.

In 2007, the theme for the holiday origami tree was fantastic creatures: mythic and real.

Angel
Ornament

This ornament is one of my favorites for traditional holiday trees. Something about the simple shapes and the way the light plays off the surface seems just right. If you adjust the size, this project can double as a tree topper!

Paper Information For the Angel I usually prefer a minimally printed paper, though sometimes the right metallic design can add a shimmer that works with the folds of the project. The ones shown here were made from an 8″ (20.5cm) sheet of paper.

ANGEL ORNAMENT

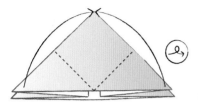 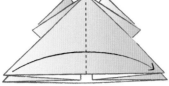 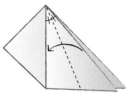

1. Start with the Waterbomb Base (page 26). Fold the bottom corners to the top.Flip over.

2. Fold in half, left to right.

3. On the front layer, fold the right side to the center.

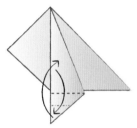 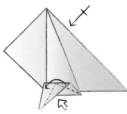 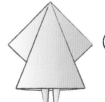 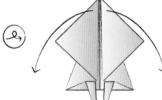

4. Fold the bottom corner up, and then back down again, but shorter than before, to create a pleat for the leg.

5.a Swivel squash fold the leg to make it narrower. Repeat steps 3–5 on the remaining long flap. Flip over.

Note: *It may help to turn the flap with the leg you just created and the remaining long flap to the left before repeating (you will have to mirror step 3).*

5.b

6. On the front layer, open the flaps.

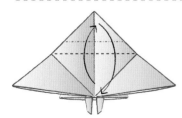 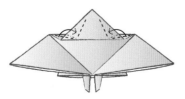 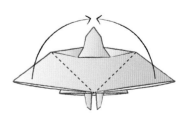

7. Fold the top corner to the bottom of the body and then up, but shorter than before, to create a pleat.

8. Inside reverse fold the bottom corners of the top triangle.

9. Fold the left and right corners along the existing creases to create wings.

MEDIUM

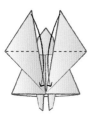

10. Fold the top of the wings to the bottom.

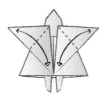

11. On the front layer, fold the bottom of the wings up. Unfold.

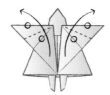

12. On the front layer, fold the bottom of the wings up between the previous crease and the edge.

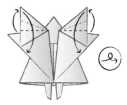

13. Fold the top corners of the wings down along the top of body and then back up, but shorter than before, to create a pleat. Flip over.

14. Fold the top corner down and to the right to create hair.

15. On the front layer, lightly fold the left and right corners toward the center to create arms.

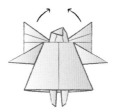

16. Pull the top corners up to open the wings.

17. Lightly fold the center of the body and mountain fold the sides of the body to shape it.

Note: *You will have to push the model from behind to round out and shape the body.*

FINISHED ANGEL ORNAMENT!

Star Light Cozy Ornament

The star light cozy is a great model because it looks nice whether you hang it on its own or assemble it into the larger modular. Either way it is subtly beautiful—it enhances your tree without stealing the show from ornaments with a lot of personality.

Paper Information For the modular shown here I used 5" (12.5cm) paper to create 3" (7.5cm) ornaments. Once the star units are combined the modular measures about 5" x 5" x 5" (12.5cm x 12.5cm x 12.5cm)

STAR LIGHT COZY UNIT (MAKE 12)

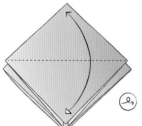 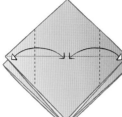 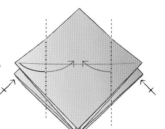 

1. Start with the Preliminary Base (page 31). On the front layer, fold in half, bottom to top. Unfold. Flip over.

2. On the front layer, fold the side corners to the center. Unfold.

3. On the front layer, inside reverse fold the left and right sides. Repeat steps 2 and 3 on the other side.

4. On the front layer, fold corner to corner in both directions. Unfold.

  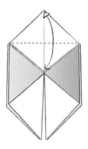 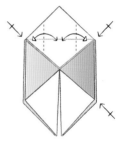

5. On the front layer, fold the bottom corner to the top.

6. On the front layer, inside reverse fold the bottom corners.

7. On the front layer, fold the top corner to the center. Unfold.

8. On the front layer, fold the sides to the center. Unfold. Repeat steps 4–8 on the remaining 3 sides.

Note: *When you stop folding and release the model, it should naturally unfold to the finished model shown here.*

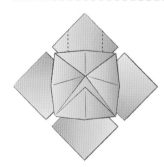

FINISHED STAR LIGHT COZY UNIT!

Note: *Make 11 more units before starting assembly. To make assembly easier, fold outer corners in. Unfold.*

STAR LIGHT COZY ASSEMBLY

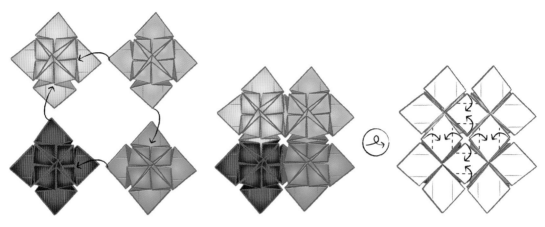

1.a Insert the tab of one star into the pocket of another. Repeat until you have 4 connected stars. Flip over.

1.b Fold the corners of the connected stars.

1.c Attach eight more stars as shown.

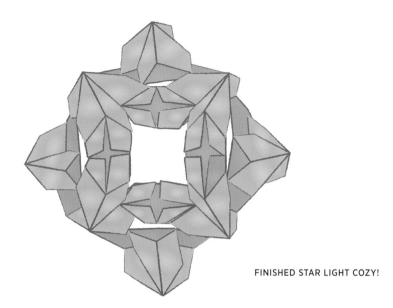

FINISHED STAR LIGHT COZY!

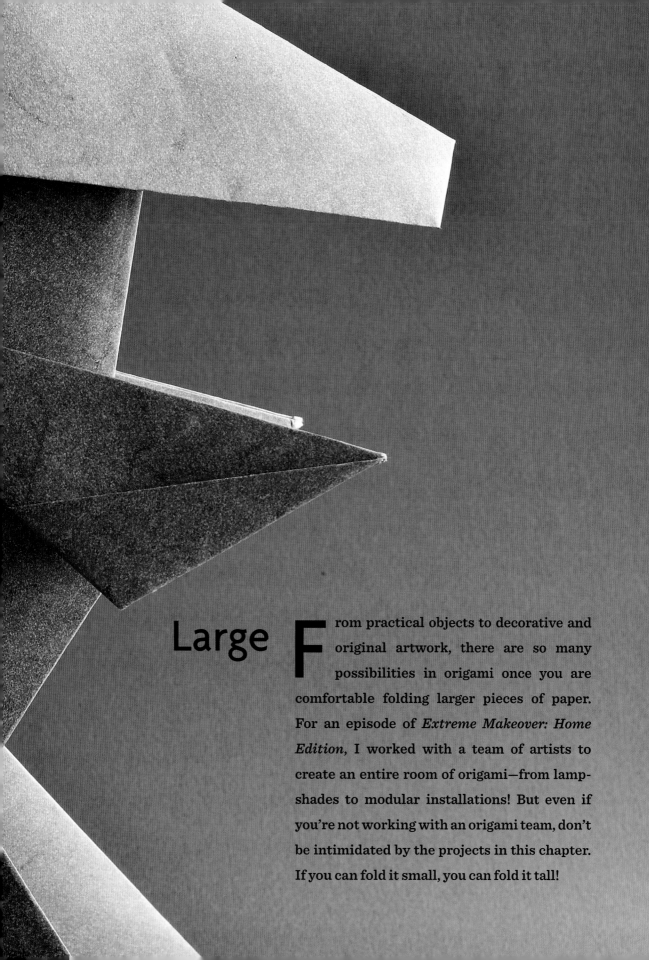

Large

From practical objects to decorative and original artwork, there are so many possibilities in origami once you are comfortable folding larger pieces of paper. For an episode of *Extreme Makeover: Home Edition*, I worked with a team of artists to create an entire room of origami—from lampshades to modular installations! But even if you're not working with an origami team, don't be intimidated by the projects in this chapter. If you can fold it small, you can fold it tall!

Subway Map Wallet

My friend Tricia and I played with various incarnations of designs until all of a sudden this wallet just happened! I was so happy with it I ended up designing an entire line of accessories using old subway maps for the New York Metropolitan Transportation Authority (MTA). You can now buy an official origami wallet at the New York Transit Museum in New York City!

Paper Information This wallet can be folded from any paper cut to 17 $\frac{1}{2}$" x 16" (44.5cm x 40.5cm), which will create a 4" x 4" (10cm x 10cm) wallet. I've found that Tyvek envelopes and laminated paper will both last for a very long time. If you want to use found paper—like an old calendar or shopping bag—you can laminate the paper or simply reinforce the joints using shelf liner or clear packing tape (see Laminate It Yourself on page 131).

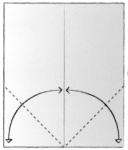

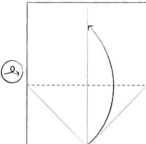

1. Fold in half, left to right, unfold.

Note: The blue square shown in the diagram is the portion of the paper that will end up on the outside of your wallet.

2. Fold the bottom corners to the center. Unfold. Flip over.

3. Fold the bottom up along the top of the diagonal creases.

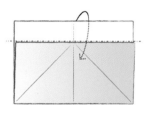

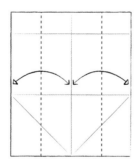

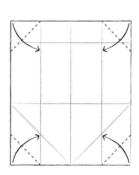

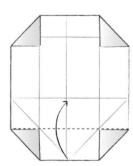

4. Mountain fold the top along the edge of the front flap. Unfold to the beginning of step 3.

5. Fold the sides to the center. Unfold.

6. Fold the corners to the previous creases.

7. Fold the bottom to the existing crease.

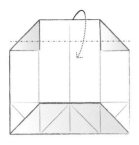 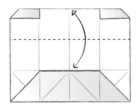 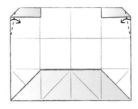 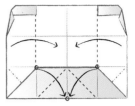

8. Mountain fold the top flap along the existing crease.

9. Fold the top to the bottom flap. Unfold.

10. Fold the top corners in.

Note: *Start the bottom point of this fold at the previous crease and make sure the top of the fold does not quite reach the top corner.*

11. Fold the sides to the center while collapsing the top corners of the front layer to the center of the bottom.

Note: *No new creases are needed for this collapse.*

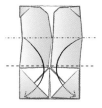

12.a Fold along the existing creases to pleat, tucking in the corners at end of the fold.

12.b

FINISHED SUBWAY MAP WALLET!

LAMINATE IT YOURSELF

Wallets take a beating! The typical guy will take his wallet in and out of his pocket many times a day, and ladies' wallets tend to float around in a handbag where they bump into all sorts of things. So if I'm using an everyday paper for a wallet, I always reinforce it first. But what if you don't have a laminating machine?

Don't worry. Clear shelf liner, found at most hardware or kitchen stores, works just as well. It's also the perfect size! The most common width for shelf liner is 18" (45.5cm). That size is ideal for this project since the Subway Map Wallet requires 17 ½" (44.5cm) of laminate to cover the back of the paper. Then you can use the remaining ½" (13mm) to reinforce the center joint and bottom corners of the wallet.

When it comes to applying any kind of laminate, it's best to measure out everything before taking the backing off the laminate. Once you've measured and cut it to size, remove the bottom edge of your laminate and apply it to the bottom edge of your paper. Slowly peel off more of the backing as you work. If you're using shelf liner, it should be repositionable as long as you don't press too hard initially.

Origami Bag

You're ready for a night out but you just can't find
the right bag to go with your outfit. . .why not
fold one using paper that matches your clothes?
This innovative accessory makes quite the
conversation piece. There is no sewing or gluing
required—just a sheet of paper and your hands!

Paper Information   Almost any size is fine, as long as the proportion is 2:1. A 24" x 48" (61cm x 122cm) piece of paper was used here, and it made a finished bag about 12" (30.5cm) wide.

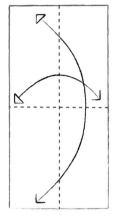

1. Fold in half, edge to edge, in both directions. Unfold.

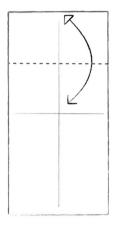

2. Fold the top to the center. Unfold.

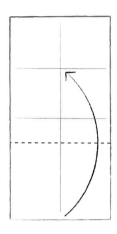

3. Fold the bottom to the top crease.

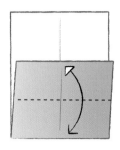

4. On the front layer, fold the top edge to the bottom. Unfold.

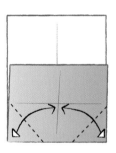

5. Fold the bottom corners to the previous crease. Unfold.

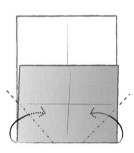

6. Inside reverse fold the bottom corners.

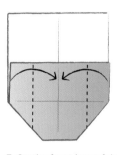

7. On the front layer, fold the sides to the center.

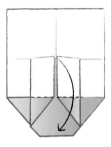

8. Fold the flap top to bottom along the existing crease.

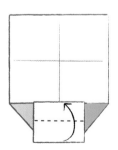

9. Fold the flap bottom to top. Unfold to the beginning of step 7.

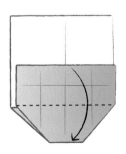

10. On the front layer, fold the top to the bottom along the bottom-most existing crease.

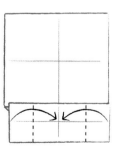

11. Fold the sides of the flap to the center.

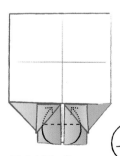

12. Fold the flap up and tuck it into the pockets to lock. Flip over.

LARGE

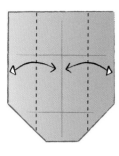

13. Fold the sides to the center. Unfold.

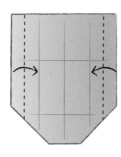

14. Fold the sides to the previous crease.

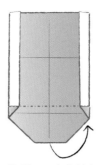

15. Mountain fold the bottom section along the top of the small triangles.

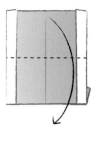

16. Fold the top down along the existing crease.

Note: *The top edge will go past the bottom edge.*

17. Fold the bottom edge up. Unfold.

18. On the front layer, fold the top to the previous crease.

19. On the front layer, fold flap down. Unfold back to the beginning of step 15.

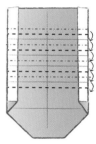

20. Pleat the existing creases bottom to top.

Note: *Start with the second crease from the top of the small triangles, which is a mountain crease.*

21.a Fold the sides in along the existing creases. Flip over.

21.b

22. Fold the top corners to the edge of the pleats.

23. Fold the top corner down.

24. Fold the top flap down to close.

FINISHED ORIGAMI BAG!

Storage Box with Lid

I came up with this box while working on a package design for a beauty-supply company. Even though this was not the design they ended up choosing, it is still one of my favorites. The entire project is folded from a single sheet—including the lid!

Paper Information The box shown here is an example of using recycled paper—it's made from a long page of an old calendar (about 12″ x 24″ [30.5cm x 61cm]). You can also make this box from a square sheet of paper, though I wouldn't recommend going under 10″ (25.5cm).

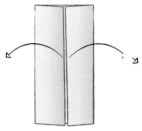

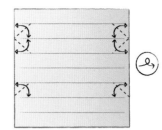

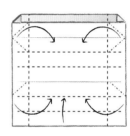

1. Start with the Cupboard Base (page 28). Unfold.

2. Fold halfway between all existing creases. Unfold. Rotate. Flip over.

3. Fold and unfold diagonally between the existing creases. Flip over.

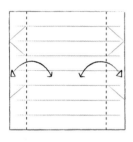
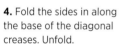

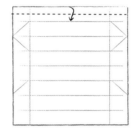

4. Fold the sides in along the base of the diagonal creases. Unfold.

5. Fold the top edge down to the nearest crease.

6. Fold the top corners to the edge of the flap.

7. Collapse along existing creases.

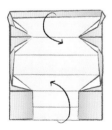

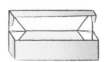

8. Fold the bottom and top in, tucking in the flap on the bottom to lock.

Note: *Push in the diagonal creases while folding in the sides at the same time. I start at the bottom and work my way up.*

FINISHED STORAGE BOX WITH LID!

Deer Head Trophy

I conceptualized this model while working on the safari-themed origami tree at the American Museum of Natural History. It was originally going to be a gazelle, but I reworked the split and shape of the antlers to turn it into a deer!

Paper Information For a deer head big enough to hang on the wall—one that is about 14″ (35.5cm)— you should start with a square piece of paper that measures 36″ (91cm).

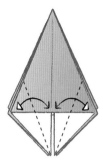

1. Start with the Frog Base (page 33). On the front layer, fold the bottom flaps to the center. Unfold.

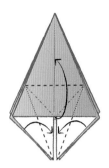

2.a Fold the bottom of the large triangle up, collapsing left and right sides to the center. This is the front. Flip over.

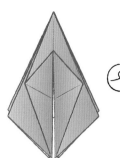

2.b

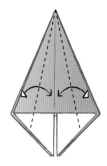

3. Fold left and right sides to the center. Unfold.

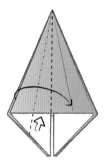

4. Open and squash fold the left flap along the existing creases.

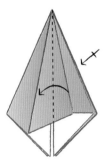

5. Move front flap from right to left. Repeat steps 4 and 5 on the right side. This is the back.

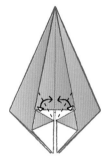

6. On the front layer, fold the bottom diagonal sides into the center. Unfold.

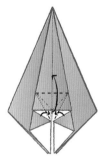

7. On the front layer, fold the bottom edge up, collapsing the left and right sides to the center.

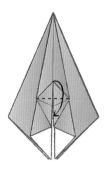

8. Fold the triangle down.

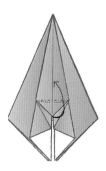

9. Tuck the flap inside.

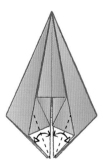

10. Fold bottom diagonal sides to center. Unfold.

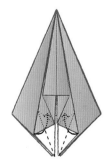

11. Inside reverse creating a new flap that meets corner to corner.

LARGE

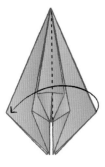

12. Move rightmost flap to the left.

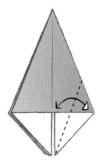

13. This is the side of the model. Fold bottom right diagonal side into center. Unfold.

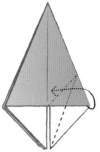
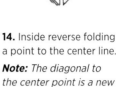

14. Inside reverse folding a point to the center line.

Note: *The diagonal to the center point is a new fold.*

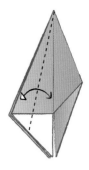

15. Fold top left diagonal side into center. Unfold.

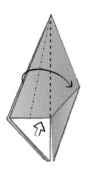

16. Open and squash fold the left flap along the previous fold lines.

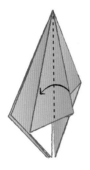

17. Move front flap from right to left.

18. Fold bottom two diagonal sides to center. Unfold.

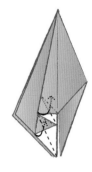

19. Inside reverse creating new flaps that meet corner to corner.

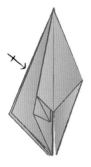

20.a This is the finished view. Repeat steps 13-19 on the other side.

Note: *There should only be one other side.*

20.b This is the finished view.

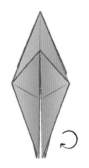

21. Flip over to the front. Rotate 180 degrees.

22. Fold triangle flap up to create the nose.

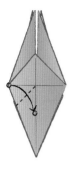
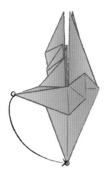

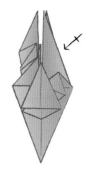

23. Fold left corner down while opening and squash folding the long top flap to the bottom.

24. On front layer, fold flap up. This is the ears. Repeat on other side.

25. Outside reverse front to finish the nose.

26. Mountain fold entire model in half.

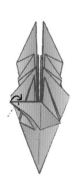

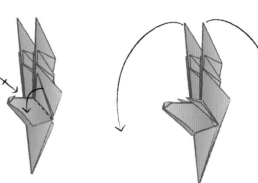

27. Fold ear flaps forward. Repeat on other side.

28. Open antlers to the sides and shape the antlers and the ears to finish.

FINISHED DEER HEAD TROPHY!

Sakura Blossom Lampshade

I designed this light fixture as a kusudama—a type of modular origami
that creates a ball, star, or orb from many different pieces. I've found
that with large-enough units, the open sides of this kusadama make it a
great lampshade for LED bulbs. Most LED lights give off no heat and
are safe to use with paper, but double-check before installing any light
inside a paper fixture. Do not use this model with a regular lightbulb! It
will heat up and create a fire hazard.

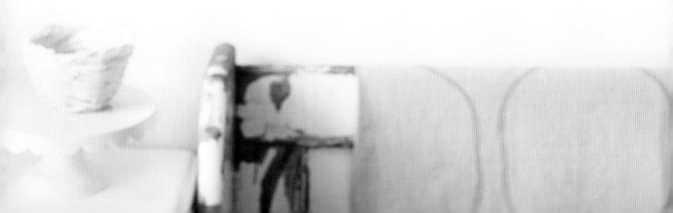

Paper Information You can find paper that has been treated to be heat- and fireproof online or at specialty art supply shops. Folding from 7" (18cm) squares will make the lampshade shown here, which is about 13" (33cm).

SAKURA UNIT (MAKE 30)

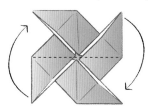

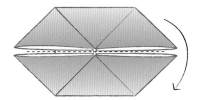

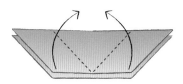

1. Start with the Windmill Base (page 30). Fold the left and right flaps in the opposite direction.

2. Mountain fold in half.

Note: *Make sure the points are separated and not trapped inside.*

3. On the front layer, fold the left and right corners up.

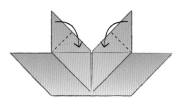

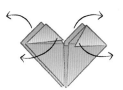

4. On the front layer, fold the top corners down.

5. Repeat steps 3 and 4 on the other side.

6. Gently open by pulling the 4 corners apart.

FINISHED SAKURA UNIT!

Note: *Fold 29 more units before starting assembly.*

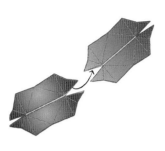
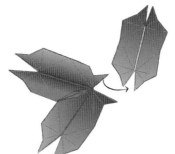
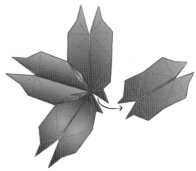

1. Insert top right flap of one unit into top left pocket of another unit to join.

Note: The full triangle flap will slide in the pocket. Once the flap is inserted make sure to push up the joint slightly to reinforce.

2.a Continue joining units until 5 units are connected.

2.b

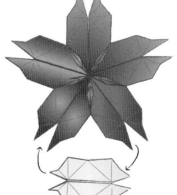

2.c

3. Connect a sixth unit to act as a "bridge" between the two clusters of 5.

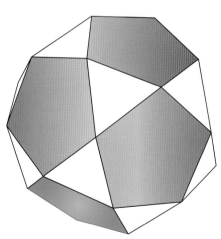

4. Continue to connect more clusters as shown to create a sphere.

FOLDING LARGER MODELS

The most common questions I am asked as an origami artist are "What is the most difficult thing you have ever folded?" and "What is the largest piece of origami you've ever done?" My answer to both questions is a 50-foot (15m) dragon with legs, wings, and three heads, made from more than 1,000 gum wrappers! Luckily I didn't have to make this monster alone. It took seventy-five people about two months, but the result was the spectacular holiday tree for the American Museum of Natural History in 2007 you see on page 117.

As that example shows, extra-large origami can be made out of many smaller pieces of paper. However, there is also big paper available. The most common paper used for oversized folding is seamless photo backdrop paper. It feels like soft card stock and tends to be delicate, but with the right model it can be breathtaking. You can find photo backdrop paper in most photography shops or online, and it's reasonably inexpensive. Of course with paper that large, it makes things easier if you have an extra pair (or two) of hands to help!

Whether you have help or not, folding oversized models is all about planning ahead. I always make sure I am so familiar with a model I can almost fold it by memory before attempting a supersized version. Being familiar with the folds helps you plan out the process and keeps you from making big mistakes.

There are a couple other differences you'll notice when you attempt your first giant piece of origami. For example, the extreme precision of a smaller model isn't always possible; you just have to relax and fold as accurately as possible. Another difference you're sure to notice is that you often must utilize your entire body to fold—almost like origami yoga!

Charlie the Dino-Squirrel

This funny creature came into existence when I tried to design a
dinosaur model with a long, substantial tail. I was playing around
with the proportions of the tail when it hit me: The model looked
more like a squirrel than a dinosaur! Since origami can be geometric
representations of any particular object, insect, or creature,
I decided I would save this silly creature. I named him Charlie, for
my brother, who can be pretty silly himself!

Paper Information This model has a long tail, almost three-fourths the size of the original piece of paper. To make a large model like the one shown on the next page, use a sheet of 42″ (1.4m) seamless backdrop paper (available at art supply shops and photo stores).

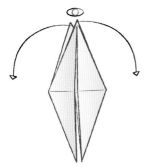

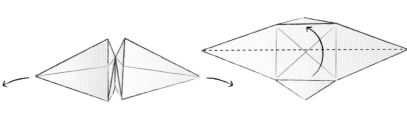

1.a Start with the Bird Base (page 32). Pull top flaps apart, opening up until the top of the model lies flat.

Note: *This modified base is called the Stretched Bird Base.*

1.b

2. Fold in half, bottom to top.

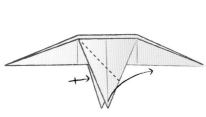

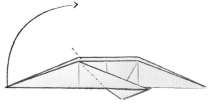

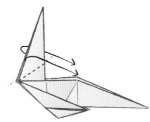

3. Fold the front flap to the right. Repeat on the other side.

4. Inside reverse fold the left side.

5. Outside reverse fold the top.

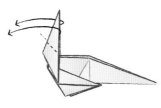

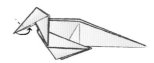

6. Inside reverse fold the left corner.

Note: *Fold both top left corners down and in.*

7. Outside reverse fold the top to create the head.

8. Tuck the left corner underneath to blunt the nose.

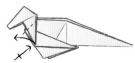

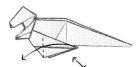

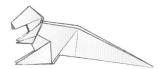

9. Fold the small flap toward the head to create an arm. Repeat on the other side.

10. Fold the large flap toward the head to create a leg. Repeat on the other side.

FINISHED DINOSAUR

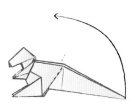

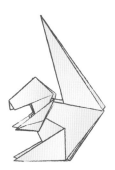

11. Inside reverse fold the right flap to create an upright tail.

FINISHED CHARLIE THE DINO-SQUIRREL!

Momma Elephant

Most models in this book can translate easily to a larger size, but I wouldn't recommend making many of them this big! The instructions for the Momma Elephant are nearly identical to the Baby Elephant (page 70), which you may have already folded, but with a couple extra creases to make things easier when you come to the end.

Paper Information This model will shrink down to about 75 percent of your starting size. In other words, if you have an 18-foot (5.5m) square of paper, you will end up with a 13½-foot (4.1m) elephant like the one shown here! However I recommend using paper no bigger than 4-feet (122cm) for an elephant that will stand well without much in the way of reinforcement.

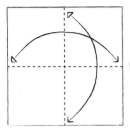 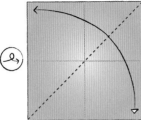 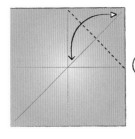 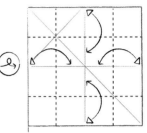

1. Fold in half, edge to edge, in both directions. Unfold. Flip over.

2. Fold the bottom right corner to the top left. Unfold.

3. Fold the top right corner to the center. Unfold. Flip over.

4. Fold all 4 sides to the center. Unfold.

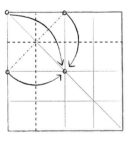 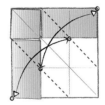 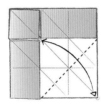 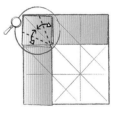

5. Collapse the top corner section (the top left corner will remain on top).

Note: You just formed an "isolated" Preliminary Base (page 31)! Origami animal models often use this isolation technique to create a more distinct separation between the head (or tail) and the body.

6. Fold the top right and bottom left corners to the existing creases. Unfold.

7. Fold the bottom right corner to the Preliminary Base. Unfold.

8.a Fold the isolated Preliminary Base into half of a Bird Base (see page 32). Flip over.

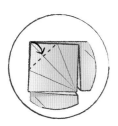

8.b

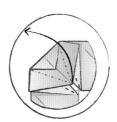

8.c

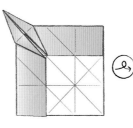

8.d

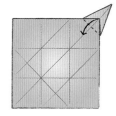

9.a On the front layer, fold the top right corner down.

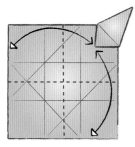

9.b

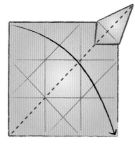

10. Fold in half, top left to bottom right. Rotate.

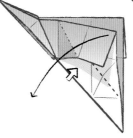

11. On the front layer, open and squash fold the top right corner.

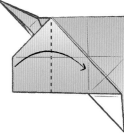

12. Fold the left edge of the flap right along the existing crease.

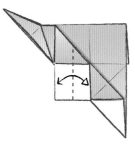

13. Fold the front layer of the flap. Unfold.

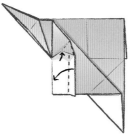

14. Inside reverse fold the flap to create the front leg.

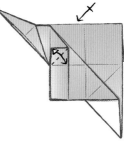

15. Fold the top left corner of the front leg down. Unfold. Repeat steps 11–15 on the other side.

16. Fold the right edge to the existing crease. Unfold.

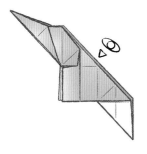

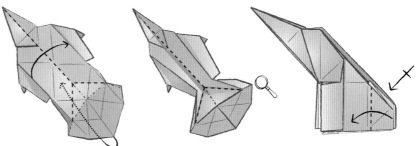

17.a View your model from the top; gently open and inside reverse from the bottom.

Note: *Tuck in the back corner while pinching the sides and closing up the model.*

17.b

17.c

18. Fold the right edge to the left, making the crease slightly to the right of the existing crease. Repeat on the other side.

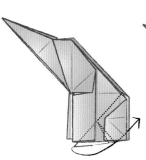

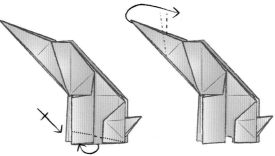

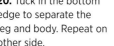

19. Inside reverse fold the flap underneath to create the tail.

20. Tuck in the bottom edge to separate the leg and body. Repeat on other side.

21. Inside reverse fold the left side of the trunk.

22. Inside reverse fold the tip of the trunk.

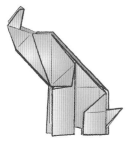

FINISHED MOMMA ELEPHANT!

TIPS

• Make sure to practice with varying degrees of sizes before attempting this bigger elephant.

• When using seamless photo backdrop papers, sometimes an overly crisp fold will make it difficult for a model to stand up at the end. It helps to make the folds firmly, but with a soft curve at points so you don't break the fibers of the paper.

• When you're folding with large paper, it is good to get some help with the preliminary folds. Trying to fold the long diagonal will be easier—and more fun!—if you have help.

Resources

NATIONAL STORES AND WEBSITES

The Container Store
www.containerstore.com
212-366-4200
I know, I know—what is the Container Store doing on this list? Surprisingly this store has a large selection of beautiful gift-wrap paper during the holidays. Of course, they also have containers to store all of your paper goods!

Dick Blick Art Materials
www.dickblick.com
800-828-4548
This art supply store carries a wide variety of paper for a wide variety of artists. If you're looking for a specific weight or archival paper, you can probably find it here.

Jo-Ann Fabrics and Crafts
www.joann.com
888-739-4120
This national retailer has a pretty nice selection of scrapbooking paper.

Kate's Paperie
www.katespaperie.com
800-809-9880
Kate's selection has some of the most varied decorative papers from around the world. The buyers keep the inventory fresh, and you'll always find new paper that is very foldable.

Michael's
www.michaels.com
800-642-4235
Another national retailer, Michael's has a large selection of scrapbooking paper as well as many other paper-related supplies.

Paper Jade
http://paperjade.com
Fine Japanese papers for origami and more are available here.

Paper Source
www.paper-source.com
888-727-9111
Their website has a wide selection of basic solids and decorative papers.

Paper Tree
www.paper-tree.com
415-921-7100
This shop, run by sisters Vicky Mihara Avery and Linda Mihara, is made for the origami artist. It's a must visit if you find yourself in San Francisco.

Pearl Paint
www.pearlpaint.com
800-451-7327
The decorative paper section at Pearl is pretty big, and they have a wide range of other art supplies.

NEW YORK STORES

A. I. Friedman
44 West 18th Street
New York, NY 10011
212-243-9000
www.aifriedman.com
This is an art supply store with lots of beautiful, decorative papers ideal for origami. They have an extended catalog of decorative papers you can order from at the paper counter.

Arthur's Invitations
15 East 13th Street
New York, NY 10003
212-807-6502
www.arthursinvitations.com
This place is a hidden treasure of a stationery store! They are one of the best independent stores and are very well stocked with beautiful papers.

Kinokuniya Bookstore
1073 Sixth Avenue
New York, NY 10036
212-869-1700
This location has the largest selection of Japanese origami paper I have seen in New York. Their selection of yuzen chiyogami papers is also quite large.

New York Central Art Supply
62 Third Avenue
New York, NY 10003
212-473-7705
www.nycentralart.com
Once you start flipping through the large boards of paper samples hung on the walls at this store, you will be overwhelmed with the quantity and quality. The staff is very knowledgeable.

Paper Presentation
23 West 18th Street
New York, NY 10011
212-463-7035
http://paperpresentation.com
A crafter's dream store with various paper options for origami, from rolls of wrapping paper to scrapbooking squares. They have a great selection of containers and boxes to organize your papers, too.

Talas
330 Morgan Avenue
Brooklyn, NY 11211
212-219-0770
www.talas-nyc.com
With professional archival, bookbinding, conservation, and restoration supplies, this business is a hidden gem. They have beautiful imported Italian, Japanese, and marbled papers as well as fabric that has been bonded to paper for bookbinding.

ORIGAMI ORGANIZATIONS AND WEBSITES

OrigamiUSA
www.origami-usa.org
OrigamiUSA is the main not-for-profit origami organization in the United States. Membership includes four issues of The Paper (an origami newsletter), discounts to special folding sessions, and access to the origami convention held each year at the Fashion Institute of Technology in New York.

British Origami Society
www.britishorigami.info
This is the biggest British origami organization. Membership includes six issues of their newsletter and access to conventions (there are two annual origami events at different locations in England).

Korea Origami Association
www.origami.or.kr
This Korean origami society is also a paper manufacturer. They have monthly meetings and newsletters.

Origamido Studio
www.origamido.com
Michael LaFosse and Richard Alexander's website is definitely worth a visit. It's filled with great information about paper and papermaking. You can order books, kits, and DVDs.

Alex Barber's Origami Diagrams
www.origami.com
Alex's website is a database of origami diagrams he's compiled for years. You can search by difficulty levels and by author.

Joseph Wu Origami
www.origami.as
Joseph has a wonderful origami website with galleries of his personal work and more. He has a great resources and links section as well.

Robert Lang Origami
www.langorigami.com
Robert is a master origami artist who has written many books. His website is an online gallery of his creations, supplemented with information about origami design challenges.

Yuri and Katrin Shumakov Oriland
www.oriland.com
The Orilands have created a world of whimsical origami. Their website is a fun fantasy world made from inventive folds.

Won Park's Money Origami
http://orudorumagi11.deviantart.com
Won is a genius dollar-bill origami artist from Canada—just look at some of his designs! He also leads a Yahoo! group for dollar-bill folders called Money Folders Unite.

Origami House Japan
www.origamihouse.jp/index.html
Makoto Yamaguchi is a Japanese origami master with dozens of books published in both Japanese and English. His website is in Japanese so you'll have to use a translation tool, but it is worth it!

Acknowledgments

Life is meaningless without lasting friendships, and there are many of you that have supported me and helped me through this long process. Thanks to Alex Horwitz for being the loving nemesis you have always been in my life. Mark Wilson for being the first to believe in me to give up the corporate ladder to become an artist—without you, Creased, Inc. would not exist. Justin Spring for your wise advice and guidance. Michael LaFosse and Richard Alexander, you guys are such an inspiration to me in so many ways. Thanks so much for everything you have done for me. The GFF (Alan Wise, Bernadette Conner, Shivani Metha) for giving me such moments of joy and laughter. Marcio Noguchi (lMNop) you always manage to bail me out of tough origami emergencies! For their expert help in the initial photography, Maya Choi, Thomas Sirgedas, and Emilie Jackson. Kally Han, thanks for your support and friendship all the way from Seoul!

To my lovely family who have supported me all my life even though I always did things a little differently. Thanks Mom and Dad for being such great parents and giving me the right morals and a strong sense of humbleness that have shaped who I am today. Chang Ui hyung and Juhui for your patience and understanding. Sok Min and Brandy for your loving support. Charlie you are my most favorite youngest brother of them all!

Thanks to everyone who helped with testing diagrams as well as with overall inspiration to write this book: Dor Jeong, Clara Onishi, Lily Tamanaha, Gay Merrill Gross, Peter Tagatac, Tricia Tait, Wendy Zeichner, Wesley Damgo, Jim Weir, Elizabeth Burgos, Freddy Burgos, John Weiss, Judy Kapner, Wenhau Chao, Shrikant Iyer, Lenora Zeitchick, Richard Logue, Kathy Knapp, Vishakaha Apte, Kathryn Wagner, Joy Low, Seth Friedman, Margeaux Snyder, Rick Burkhardt.

Special thanks also to Leonardo Pignataro, Shrikant Iyer, the Bean Girls and family, Ingrid, JaeHee, Mrs. Rho, and the Lucky Bird Club.

Last but not least, I'd like to thank the wonderful team at Potter Craft: Betty Wong for making this book possible, Chi Ling Moy for her sophisticated eye, and Thom O'Hearn for being such a gentle and giving soul when it came to the editing of this book. I don't know how I could have made it through this without your encouragement, guidance, and support!

About the Author

SOK SONG's passion for origami transformed his self-taught hobby into an award-winning design business. His paper artistry has been featured in magazines including *Vanity Fair, Marie Claire, GQ,* and *Vogue;* as contributions to other origami books; on TV including *Extreme Makeover: Home Edition* and *America's Next Top Model;* and in museums including the American Museum of Natural History. **Visit his website at www.creased.com.**

Index

Note: Page numbers in *italics* indicate projects